HOW WE GET OUR ENGLISH BIBLE

Understanding About Different Versions

ROBERT E. PICIRILLI

randall house
114 Bush Rd | Nashville, TN 37217
randallhouse.com

© 2019 by Robert E. Picirilli

Published by Randall House Publications
114 Bush Road
Nashville, TN 37217

All rights reserved. No part of this publication may be reproduced, stored in a retrieval system, or transmitted in any form or by any means—electronic, mechanical, photocopy, recording, or any other means—except for brief quotation in critical reviews, without the prior permission of the publisher.

Printed in the United States of America

13-ISBN 9781614841050

Table of Contents

Preface v

Chapter 1
What We Believe About the Bible 1

Chapter 2
**Bridging the Gap: How the Original Bible Comes to Us,
Part I: Copying and Publishing** 9

Chapter 3
**Bridging the Gap: How the Original Bible Comes to Us.
Part II: Translations** 21

Chapter 4
**The Bible in the Language of the People: The Original Text
and the Goal of Translations** 39

Chapter 5
**What You Need to Know About the English
of the King James** 51

Chapter 6
The Original Preface to the King James Version 71

Chapter 7
Translation: Understanding How It Works 85

Chapter 8
What about Manuscript Differences? 99

Chapter 9
**Confidence in Our Bibles: The Providence of God
and the Preservation of His Word** 121

Chapter 10
Some Practical Suggestions 131

Preface

Many Christians are distressed about different versions of the Bible. They hear various people—some they know, some they don't—say all sorts of things back and forth, perhaps claiming that only this or that version is really the Word of God. They feel threatened, fearful that they will somehow lose their contact with the Word of God if they make the wrong choices.

Perhaps I am foolish to think I might be able to help you understand the things that are involved in our having different versions of the Bible. Foolish or not, that is my only desire: to increase understanding. If this little book is helpful, then I can think that perhaps our Lord led me to undertake this project. If not, I'll know it was my own decision.

My purpose is not to enter into anyone's debate about versions. I will offer no *arguments* for or against any certain view. I will say nothing critical of those who hold any view. And I certainly don't aim to try to persuade anyone in favor of or against a given version. I can't imagine, for example, why anyone would want to turn people away from the King James Version, which has served English-speaking people well for 400 years.

All I want to do is provide the kind of information that will help you understand how the Bible has come (and continues to come) to us. Many wonderful things have transpired, and you need to understand them. There are many things at play in the different translations—not just English but hundreds of languages around the world.

My feeling is that if people understand what's involved, they can make up their own minds about what version or versions they can use and still be confident they have the Word of God in their hands. The difference is that they will be making their decisions intelligently, in light of knowing what's involved, rather than simply taking someone's word for things. Surely this is the way of wisdom.

I am writing informally, as though I am talking directly to others in my presence. I will write in the first person and address the reader as *you*—which is not usually approved for publishing.

I am also avoiding technical terminology, as much as possible. Now and then I will provide the technical terms in footnotes, but you can skip those, if you wish, and still get the point.

I am writing for *my* people, those of the denomination that has raised me. These are the people I know best—and who know me best. I am primarily concerned about them, although if others find this book useful, I am gratified.

You should know that I make no pretense of being a textual scholar. The textual scholars[1] are a relatively small group of people who, in summary, compare the various manuscripts, passage by passage, to see where they differ and try to determine which manuscripts have the original wording. But I understand what's involved in this work and I believe you too can understand enough to see how the manuscript differences affect all versions of the Bible.

For that matter, I am not a scholar at all. I have done a few "scholarly" things, but the best that can be said is that I have played around the edges of scholarship a little. My gifts, I believe, lie more toward understanding things and teaching. This book, like all those I have written, is one way I try to teach.

---

[1] Often called "textual critics," using *critics/criticism* in the sense of critically analyzing the different wordings and making judgments or decisions about them.

I sincerely hope you will find that this book helps you understand how we get our Bibles, why we have different versions of the Bible, and how to evaluate those differences and still rejoice in having the Word of God—where you meet Him and hear Him speak to you.

I wish to offer a special thanks to the Wednesday morning Bible study group and pastoral staff at Cofer's Chapel, who graciously permitted me to "test" this material on them during nine Wednesday mornings. They offered wise counsel and helpful suggestions. After each session, I came back home and made refinements to what I had already written. I'm privileged to be part of that group of seniors.

Thanks also to Dr. James Leonard (a New Testament scholar) and Dr. Matthew McAffee (an Old Testament scholar) for reading the manuscript and providing numerous helpful suggestions. The opinions in this work, however, are mine, and they would not agree with everything I have said.

Chapter One
What We Believe About the Bible

Before I get into the differences in versions and what lies behind them, I want to put down a foundation for everything else in this book.

This chapter states what we believe about the Bible as inspired by God. In my mind, I am stating what all Bible-believing Christians teach about the Bible. This confidence is what counts above all else.

Nothing later in this book will contradict what's in this chapter. If any reader *thinks* something in another chapter contradicts what's in this one, then either I have failed to make what I say clear enough or the reader has misunderstood me.

We Believe in the *Plenary, Verbal Inspiration* of the Bible

I am violating my promise not to use technical terminology in this instance for a reason. I want to introduce the traditional, Bible-believing terminology for the Christian view of inspiration.

The word *plenary* means full and complete. When we use this word in expressing our view of the Bible, we mean that inspiration applies to *all* the Bible, to every single part of it, to all sixty-six books (thirty-nine in the Old Testament, twenty-seven in the New Testament). And we mean that all of the inspired Word of God is there. Nothing is missing.

The word *verbal* focuses on the words. By using *verbal* in naming our view of inspiration, we are saying that inspiration extends to all the words chosen. Some people think the Bible is inspired in a more general way, and that only the basic ideas can be trusted as having God's own authority behind them. But we believe in the divine authority of every single word, each one chosen under the influence of the Holy Spirit. After all, the accuracy of the communication of any idea depends on the words used to express that idea.

So when we say we believe in the plenary-verbal inspiration of the Bible we mean that all of it is inspired by God, including the very words used.

Which leads me to a definition.

The Meaning of Inspiration as Applied to the Bible

Sometimes people use *inspire* or *inspiration* in a very broad sense to mean being influenced in a positive way about almost anything. These days, the NBC Nightly News often names its final segment as "Inspiring America."

But when applied to the Bible, *inspiration* has a very special and unique meaning.

Second Timothy 3:16 says, simply enough, "All Scripture is given by inspiration of God." The last five words in this statement, "given by inspiration of God," translate just one Greek word which literally means "God-breathed." The whole Bible, then, is the breath of God.

When He was tempted by Satan, Jesus quoted Deuteronomy 8:3: "Man shall not live by bread alone, but by every word that proceeds out of the mouth of God." Words come from a person's mouth, and so they are one's very breath. When the Lord created Adam, He made a form from clay and then *breathed* into that form, and Adam became a living soul (Gen. 2:7). Just as physical life depends on the breath of

God, so our spiritual lives depend on the breath of the Spirit of God as manifested in the words of Holy Scripture.

How do we define inspiration, then? Here's the traditional, Bible-believing way of doing that. Inspiration is a work of the Holy Spirit performed on those who wrote the Bible. It means that when those human authors wrote, they did so under the controlling influence of the Spirit who guided them. In all the effort they put into the writing—whether thinking, researching, dictating, or writing—they were so superintended by the Spirit of God that what they wrote was exactly what God wanted to say. And this activity included the very words they chose to express themselves.

When Paul wrote 2 Timothy 3:16, saying all Scripture is given by inspiration of God, he might have been thinking of the Old Testament in particular. But the Bible-believing Christian view is that this verse *applies* just as much to the New Testament as to the Old Testament.

And here's an important point. The Bible-believing position on this doctrine is that inspiration was a very special, unique influence exercised on the human authors of the sixty-six books we identify as the Bible,[2] and *on them alone*! Such inspiration has not been at work on any persons who write or speak (or otherwise express themselves) since the Bible was completed.

We Believe the Bible Is a Divine-Human Book

This statement simply means that both God and man were actively at work. Here's a good place to bring in 2 Peter 1:20-21: "… No prophecy of the scripture is of any private interpretation. For the

---

[2] These sixty-six books are often called the *canon*, a word that originally means a rule or standard and then comes to identify the settled content of the Bible as a whole.

prophecy came not in old time by the will of man: but holy men of God spake as they were moved by the Holy Ghost."

Understand, first, that this verse is referring to *all* Scripture as prophetic.

Next, understand that "is of private interpretation" refers to the manner in which the Scriptures came about, as the next line shows in its explanation. None of the prophetic Scriptures came into existence as a result of any individuals' reading of events or as a result of the human authors' will to write that came from within themselves.

Most important, understand then just how the prophetic Scriptures *did* come about: "Holy men of God (the human authors) spoke (wrote) as they were moved (literally, carried or borne along) by the Holy Spirit."

So the Bible is the work of human beings, in one sense—although not of them alone. There were human authors, and for many of the books the human authors are identified. *Men ... spoke.* They acted as any human writer would act, and that could include interviewing witnesses and checking facts as well as deciding what to include and how to say it. Luke 1:1-4 is helpful in understanding this idea.

The human authors wrote in their own unique styles. In the Greek originals, the style and language usage of Luke is very different, for example, from that of John. If you understand that three different preachers may preach the same text in their own styles, and yet agree on what God has said, you can understand this difference in the human authors of Scripture.

But at the same time the human beings were actively engaged in their work, the Holy Spirit was also actively engaged, leading and guarding them so every interview and every decision they made yielded the very words God wanted said. This was a *supernatural* (use "miraculous" if you wish) work. As men worked, prompted by God, God worked in and through them.

Biblical theologians often insist that Jesus Christ was (and is) a *God-man*, fully human and fully divine. Somewhat parallel to this doctrine of the person of Christ, the Bible is a divine-human work. God spoke, men spoke (wrote). And God worked in such a way that the final product was His life-giving, saving Word, in every aspect and particular.

Along these lines consider this: in many parts of the Bible the human author identifies himself. For one of many examples, take Romans 1:1-7: "Paul, a servant of Jesus Christ ... to all that be in Rome." If Paul were not the author of the work, he would be deceiving us in claiming to be. (You can be sure that my secretary never claimed that a letter I dictated to her was from her!) One may even say that the Holy Spirit led Paul to claim to be the author. Even so, the Holy Spirit was the author.

The Bible Is Inerrant

Flowing logically from what I've just said is this, then: if God is the author (in and behind the human authors), and if God cannot err (as He cannot, by definition), then the Bible does not express anything erroneous as so. It leads us into no mistakes but always speaks truth.

Sure, the Bible records the mistakes that people make and the errors they state. It reveals to us, for example, that fools say there is no God (Psa. 14:1). But the Bible does not make any erroneous statements of fact. God cannot lie (Heb. 6:18).

It is important, these days, to add this insistence, on the inerrancy of Scripture, to the way we express our doctrine of the Bible itself. Some people try to claim the *inspiration* of the Bible and yet allow for it to be mistaken in limited ways. They may say, for example, that the Bible can err in matters of history or science without erring in what it teaches about salvation and Christian living.

But the doctrine of inerrancy, which we who are Bible-believing Christians profess, insists that the Bible contains no errors in anything it intends to communicate, whether in matters of history or science or anything else. In other words, whatever the Bible affirms to be so, is so.

A Matter of Our Faith

I should conclude this brief chapter by emphasizing that our view of Scripture is a matter of faith.

In saying this, I do not mean to say there are no good reasons for believing this, or that there is no good evidence to sustain this belief. I am satisfied that both reasons and evidence exist. The claims of Scripture, its coherence (that it makes sense as a whole), and its effectiveness in our lives and the lives of others—all these and more are convincing in this regard.

And it doesn't hurt that many things once thought to be mistakes in the Bible have since been shown to be accurate.

And, although my purpose here does not include defending our doctrine, we are always willing to do so by giving reasons and citing evidence (1 Pet. 3:15).

But, in the end, like saving faith, our faith in the Bible as the very Word of God, inspired and infallible, is a matter between us and the Lord Himself. His Spirit has influenced us and we have found in the Bible a sure foundation for our lives. As we have breathed what was breathed in those holy men of old, we have been assured that it is the breath of life and truth.

A High View of the Bible

You will recognize that what I have expressed in this chapter, as brief as it is, represents a high view of the Bible as the very Word of God.

Some of our critics have snuffed at this view and said we worship the Bible when we ought to worship God. I snuff at that! I do not worship the Bible, but when I worship God, He speaks to me in the words of the Bible and I cling to them as one who clings for dear life to the line that has been thrown to him in the raging sea.

I worship Jesus as my Lord and Savior, but the only Jesus I know is clothed in the garments of Holy Scripture.

Nail this truth down, then, as the starting point. Everything else flows from it.

Conclusion

I conclude by repeating, in a way, what I said at the beginning. There is nothing I will say, in the rest of this book, that I believe will contradict what I have said here about the Bible. I don't claim to be infallible, of course, and it is possible that I have contradicted myself without realizing it. But I think that those who carefully analyze what is to follow will be able to see how those things fit, like light bulbs in lamps, into this high view of the Bible as the Word of God.

Indeed, I believe that a full understanding of all the things involved in how our Bible has come, and continues to come, to us will increase our appreciation for the far-reaching and dynamic truth that the Bible is the Word of God.

That leaves just one all-important question: what *Bible* are we talking about? There are many and they aren't exactly alike.

Answering that question is what the rest of this book is about.

CHAPTER TWO
Bridging the Gap: How the Original Bible Comes to Us
Part I: Copying and Publishing

We've established, in chapter one, that the Bible is the inspired Word of God. All Bible-believing Christians accept this view. It is important, next, to make sure we understand what this truth means. Sometimes people misunderstand the implications.

We can be sure that the Bibles in our hands give us what the original, inspired writings said, and I'll have more to say about this confidence later. But there is a lot that has gone on between then and now, which I want to talk about in this chapter and the next. Moses and Paul, and the other human authors of the Bible, wrote down (or dictated to scribes to write down; see Rom. 16:22) the words God inspired them to write. They wrote them by hand on the kind of materials that were available to them. But, as you know, we don't hold *those* original writings in our hands.[3] They don't still exist. We are

---

[3]These are often called *autographs*.

thousands of years away from them, not to mention the difference in languages and publishing.

Moses and Isaiah wrote in the Hebrew language. Paul and Luke and John wrote in Greek. They and their scribes wrote the inspired message down on a kind of paper made from the split stalks of papyrus plants. And they wrote them by hand. So when you say that what Paul wrote to the Galatians, for example, is the inspired Word of God, don't forget what He wrote: handwritten, in the Greek language, on papyrus, with a sharpened reed as a pen, using ink with soot for its base. That isn't exactly what we hold in our hands, even though the *content* is the same.

Imagine that I could hand you a page of the Bible Paul wrote, the inspired Word of God. I can't, but imagine it anyway. If I could, it might look similar to the page in this picture—which is a handwritten copy of a page from the N.T., and it's in Greek. So what Tertius—his name means *third*, by the way—wrote to the Romans might have looked somewhat like this.

I trust you see my point. What God inspired Paul to dictate to Tertius is the original form of the Word of God. All I'm saying is that there is a significant distance between the original writings and you and me. We need to know how to fill in that gap so we understand the confidence I mentioned above.

There are two main things standing between the originals and us.

But before I get to those two, start with this as a foundation to build on: the original hand-written text of Matthew, Mark, Luke, and

John, or the letters of Paul, or any of the rest of the Old or New Testaments *does not still exist anywhere in the world*—so far as we know.

Don't exaggerate this fact. In a way it doesn't matter. There are enough early copies, also handwritten (more or less like the one in the picture), that we can be very confident we know exactly what the originals had in them, with very little room for difference of opinion. In other words, we may not have the original sheets, but we have the original *text*, found in the abundance of manuscripts that exist. And the places where there remain any differences of opinion make absolutely no difference for Christian doctrine or practice. I'll come back to this point often, because it is very, very important.

Anyway, we don't have the original copies, and it would be foolish of us to tell our non-Christian friends that we do. They would soon find out the truth, and then they wouldn't trust anything else we told them about the Bible.

OK, that brings me to the two things that stand between the originals and us. Those two things are (1) the *copying* of the Bible; and (2) the *translating* of the Bible. Both of those things had to take place, in many stages and large amounts over long periods of time, for us to have the Bible.

These two things are the subjects of this chapter and the following one: in this chapter, copying and publishing; in the next, translating.

Copying the Bible by Hand

First, then, to the copying that bridges the gap between what the Bible writers originally wrote and the Bibles we hold in our hands. For the first 1500 years, the copying of the Scriptures was done by hand. For the last 500 years, that copying has been done by printing presses.

Have you thought about how long 1500 years is? That's fifteen centuries. Maybe 60 generations. By comparison, people of European descent have been in America less than 400 years.

(Hey, my great-great-grandfather, Redding Moore, moved from North Carolina to South Carolina in 1816 and founded the first churches of our Free Will Baptist denomination in that state. That's five generations from him to me, and there are already three more generations after me! That's eight generations in the space of 200 years!)

We call the hand-written copies *manuscripts*, a word I'll be using often in this book. It's not really a "technical term," it simply means "hand-written."[4] Fifteen hundred years is a long time for the Bible to be copied by hand from one generation to another. Older copies wore thin and needed to be replaced. Demand increased as the church spread and congregations multiplied.

No doubt there were hundreds of people, perhaps thousands, during those 1500 years, who made handwritten copies of part or all of the Bible. It was laborious work, done with quills dipped in inkwells and writing on papyrus or parchment.

Most—but not all—of the copying was done by semi-professional people, men and women who lived in the service of the church and spent hours on end copying the Bible by hand. We call them scribes or copyists. And, yes, there were women, as well as men, who did this work. Nuns and monks, often, cloistered away in the great monasteries of the established church, whether the Roman Catholics in Western Europe or the Greek Orthodox in Eastern Europe and the Mideast. (I won't take time for a chapter on church history!)

Sometimes in copying the Scriptures (and other writings) they worked with writing desks. Before that, they usually copied with the

---

[4]*Manuscript* is from the Latin, where *manu* means "by hand" and *scriptus* means "written."

writing material in their laps. Sometimes they worked as individuals, looking to the text and then writing it down—and often could write a lot of it from memory. Often they worked in groups, with someone reading aloud slowly and the scribes dutifully writing down what they heard.

The Nature of the Copyists' Work and Differences in the Copies

The process I've described above could have its problems, of course. I'll return to these problems in a later chapter. For now I want to acknowledge what we find and what your common sense will probably tell you. The copies are not all alike. They are very much alike in all the important ways, and this agreement came about because, for the most part, those making the copies took great pains to do the work carefully. Even so, there are differences in the manuscripts. Most differences are inconsequential. Only a few have any significance at all, and even then they don't affect Christian doctrine or practice.

Still, the differences show us what we would already have guessed: namely, the copyists were not inspired. And that doesn't surprise us: *Bible-believing Christian doctrine has always limited supernatural inspiration to the original writers; we do not claim that the scribes were inspired, or even that that they were in some way supernaturally preserved from making mistakes in their work.* As I said, the differences in the copies show that this was the case.

Examining the thousands of manuscripts shows clearly that the multiplied numbers of people who made handwritten copies of the Bible during those 1500 years were human beings at work. The copies they made have differences in them. They did their best, and they did very well. But we still have to sort out the differences and determine which words matched the original, inspired text. The copies give us the inspired Word of God, but only when they match the original, inspired text. They usually do—but not always.

Yes, God has preserved His Word. One of the ways He did so was in using careful copyists—not by miraculously making all the copies just alike but by giving us enough copies so we can almost always tell exactly what the original text said.

There are thousands of Greek manuscripts of the Bible, in part or in whole, made during those 1500 years. They're in libraries and archives and monasteries and other places around the world, and they've been examined closely, photographed, and studied. The point is this: not any two of those manuscripts of any substantial size are exactly alike, word for word and letter for letter! That's not the way God worked; there are many obvious differences in the manuscripts.

Let me be quick to emphasize that these differences do *not* mean your Bible is not trustworthy. It's important to know there are enough copies in existence that those who study the manuscripts can usually determine exactly what mistakes the scribes made in their copying. Most differences in manuscripts are of little or no significance and do not affect the Christian faith. I will discuss and illustrate this matter in a later chapter.

For now, then, my point is this: *the scribes, even though they were not inspired or supernaturally preserved from errors as the original authors were, were used by God through 1500 years to preserve His Word.* As I've explained in chapter one, the human authors of the Bible wrote under a supernatural superintendence by the Holy Spirit. They made absolutely no mistakes; every word they used was chosen under the Spirit's influence, and was the very word God Himself was speaking through them. All Bible-believing Christians affirm this view of Scripture.

But the fact that the manuscripts we have do not all entirely agree means the scribes did *not* work under that special influence. Those who made hand-written copies did their work *as human beings.* Like all human beings they were imperfect. At the same time, among both the Jewish scribes who made copies of the Old Testament and the church scribes later on, there was a high regard for the Scriptures and many extraordinary precautions were taken to do their very best to ensure that the copies were accurate. The differences in the copies—as I have said and will say often—do not affect any article of Christian faith or practice.

In other words, God spoke *directly* through Isaiah and Peter, and He has preserved that Word through many, many people, over 1500 years, who made hand-written copies of it, *working as human beings under His providential oversight*. It's obvious to everyone, I think, that these copyists did not possess the same authority as the writing prophets and apostles. (It might even be scary to think that they did!)

Copying by Printing

In addition to the 1500 years when the Bible was "published"—and thus passed down to us—in many generations of handwritten copies, there are 500 more years when the copies we have were made by printing presses. But even printing presses are run by human beings, ordinary human beings who make mistakes just as you and I make mistakes. For that matter, I assume that not all the typesetters and proofreaders and pressmen in modern publishing houses that print Bibles are Christians. Even so, whether they are Christians or not, we trust them to be careful to give us the Word of God accurately, even though they are not inspired or supernaturally prevented from making mistakes. In this work, too, there are thousands of people who have made copies of the Scriptures for us.

I know that the printing process helps keep the text secure and consistent. Even so, there have been mistakes made in printing Bibles, some of them downright embarrassing. In 1631, Robert Barker and Martin Lucas, of the royal printers in London, printed an edition of the King James Bible that accidentally left the word *not* out of the seventh commandment. So the Bible was actually published, saying, "Thou shalt commit adultery!" This edition of the Bible is often called "The Wicked Bible," and one can see why.

Sure, it's a typographical error, as we call such a thing, and it doesn't trouble us. But it's an error nonetheless. Still, in print there are far less differences than in handwritten copies of the Scriptures.

By the way, you probably know that the chapter and verse divisions in our Bibles were not in the original. The present chapter divisions go back, for the most part, to the early thirteenth century; the verse divisions in common use came into being in the mid-sixteenth century in printings of the Greek New Testament. Also, the originals had very little punctuation; present punctuation has come about in various stages.

Differences in the King James

By the way, I trust you understand that not all King James Bibles are alike. On the next page, I'm including a copy of the first page of Genesis of the original King James as published in 1611, large enough that I think you can read it (not quite as large as the original). Perhaps you'll find it interesting to notice the differences in type that make it hard to read. (What's that "Chap. j" at the top of the page? What sort of word is "Alfo"?)

And there are differences in spelling (I like the "Sunne, Moone, and Starres"!) and punctuation.

Sure, these aren't earthshaking. We understand them. But anyone who feels he or she has to have every letter of every word exactly the same in order to be confident that the Bible is the Word of God should see that such an idea won't quite work—not even for the King James.

THE FIRST BOOKE OF MOSES,
called GENESIS.

CHAP. I.

1 The creation of Heauen and Earth, 3 of the light, 6 of the firmament, 9 of the earth separated from the waters, 11 and made fruitfull, 14 of the Sunne, Moone, and Starres, 20 of fish and fowle, 24 of beasts and cattell, 26 of Man in the Image of God. 29 Also the appointment of food.

Psal.33.6. and 136.5. acts.14.15. and 17.24. hebr.11.3.

IN the beginning God created the Heauen, and the Earth. 2 And the earth was without forme, and voyd, and darkenesse was vpon the face of the deepe: and the Spirit of God mooued vpon the face of the waters.

2.Cor. 4.6.

3 And God said, *Let there be light: and there was light.

4 And God saw the light, that it was good: and God diuided ‡ the light from the darkenesse.

‡ *Hebr. betweene the light and betweene the darkenesse.*
† *Hebr. and the euening was, and the morning was &c.*
* *Psal. 136. 5. Ier. 10.12 and 51.15.*
‡ *Hebr. Expansion.*

5 And God called the light, Day, and the darknesse he called Night: † and the euening and the morning were the first day.

6 ¶ And God said, *Let there be a ‡ firmament in the midst of the waters: and let it diuide the waters from the waters.

7 And God made the firmament; and diuided the waters, which were vnder the firmament, from the waters, which were aboue the firmament: and it was so.

8 And God called the *firmament, Heauen: and the euening and the morning were the second day.

Ier.51.15.

9 ¶ And God said, *Let the waters vnder the heauen be gathered together vnto one place, and let the dry land appeare: and it was so.

Psal.33.7. and 136.5. iob.38.8.

10 And God called the dry land, Earth, and the gathering together of the waters called hee, Seas: and God saw that it was good.

11 And God said, Let the Earth bring foorth † grasse, the herbe yeelding seed, and the fruit tree, yeelding fruit after his kinde, whose seed is in it selfe, vpon the earth: and it was so.

† *Heb. tender grasse.*

12 And the earth brought foorth grasse, and herbe yeelding seed after his kinde, and the tree yeelding fruit, whose seed was in it selfe, after his kinde: and God saw that it was good.

13 And the euening and the morning were the third day.

14 ¶ And God said, Let there bee *lights in the firmament of the heauen, to diuide † the day from the night: and let them be for signes and for seasons, and for dayes and yeeres.

Deu.4.19 psal.136.7.
† *Hebr. betweene the day and betweene the night.*

15 And let them be for lights in the firmament of the heauen, to giue light vpon the earth: and it was so.

16 And God made two great lights: the greater light ‡ to rule the day, and the lesser light to rule the night: he made the starres also.

‡ *Hebr. for the rule of the day, &c.*

17 And God set them in the firmament of the heauen, to giue light vpon the earth:

18 And to * rule ouer the day, and ouer

Ier.31.35

Actually, the differences are much more than in typefaces. The original King James in 1611, for example, included the Apocrypha, several books and parts of books in the Old Testament that we believe are not even part of the inspired Word of God.

Furthermore, there were several editions of the King James, with various revisions, most of them relatively unimportant. Some of these editions were in 1617, 1628, 1632, 1743, 1762, and 1769. Today's "King James" is about the same as this last one. Many of the changes were corrections of typesetting errors, although some seem to be actual textual changes. For example, in Psalm 69:32 the original said, "seek good," whereas it should have read "seek God," corrected in 1617. In 2 Corinthians 11:32, the 1611 had, simply, "the city," which was corrected in 1629 to "the city of the Damascenes." There are several of these, where different words are involved.

For that matter, there were two 1611 printings, apparently from the very same publishers and produced on the same presses. And there are numerous differences between the two.

Indeed, there are two "traditions" of the King James still in use today, one from the Oxford Press and one from the Cambridge Press, both in England and going back centuries. There aren't a lot of textual differences, but there are some. In the Oxford King James, Jeremiah 34:16 says, "whom *he* had set at liberty," which is "whom *ye* had set at liberty" in the Cambridge King James. In 2 Chronicles 33:19, the Oxford says "all his *sins*," and the Cambridge has "all his *sin*." In Nahum 3:16, the Oxford says the cankerworm "*fleeth* away," while the Cambridge has "*flieth* away." Certainly these aren't all that important, but they are differences in words.

(I understand that those who advocate for the King James only position say that it is the Oxford tradition that gives us the 100% correct Word of God, not the Cambridge tradition. But there are lots of folks, in America as well as in England (and other countries), who have the Cambridge King James.)

There are other publishers' differences, like spellings and capitalization. Some use "throughly" and some "thoroughly." Sometimes in a sermon, I call attention to the uncapitalized *holy* in *holy Spirit* in several New Testament verses, as in Ephesians 4:30, for example. I do so to emphasize that in such instances *holy* is an adjective that describes the Spirit of God as a holy being, all the more reason for us to be holy and not grieve Him. At various times, I've had people come to me afterward and say they didn't understand what I meant, because *their* King James had a capital H.

Please understand. I am not saying that all these differences in the various editions of the King James are important for the subject of this book. They aren't. They don't nullify the consistency and validity of the King James in any way.

But what they *do* show is that the work of copying the Scriptures, in modern printing as in earlier hand-copying, is not carried out under inspiration and divine protection from making mistakes. Scribes who copy by hand make errors, and the manuscripts show it. Typesetters and proofreaders make errors, and the printed editions show it. But they don't shake our confidence in the Bible as the Word of God.

Human Work Again

The publishing of the Scriptures, in whatever way they are brought to us from the originals, is human work performed under the providential hand of God as one way He has preserved His Word. He spoke directly through "holy men of God ... [who] were moved [that is, borne along] by the Holy Ghost." And for 2,000 years His Word has been published in one way or another, whether through scribes writing with pen and ink or printers setting type and running presses.

These are simply the facts. Between the original Scriptures written by the inspired writers and us, are human beings at work, copying—in one way or another—the Scriptures. Lots of them were good, godly folk, doing their work as carefully and conscientiously as they could. Some of them might not have been. And that doesn't matter, because we can tell that the Bibles in our hands give us God's Word as He originally gave it to the writing prophets and apostles.

Through it all, God preserved His Word, and we have absolutely no reason to be in doubt about what He has said to us. But He did that through human beings working in their human frailty.

Thankfully, there are many copies to provide us with adequate resources for comparison. There were many godly people involved in the process of copying and publishing. We human beings can usually spot and correct any mistakes they made. And in those relatively few places where we may not be 100% certain which of two wordings matches the original, there are no differences that would change any item of Christian doctrine or practice.

This basic agreement reassures us. God has spoken, and we have what He said, His Word. He still speaks to us in and through this Word.

In the previous chapter, I emphasized that our confidence in the Bible as the inspired Word of God is a matter of our *faith*. Likewise, the fact that He has preserved His Word through the 2,000 years since Christ came, and well beyond that since the time of Moses, is also a matter of our faith. His two kinds of work—inspiration of the original writers and providential preservation through all the human work involved in bringing that inspired Word to us in our Bibles—are beliefs that have stood the test of time and been reinforced by convincing evidence.

CHAPTER THREE
Bridging the Gap: How the Original Bible Comes to Us
Part II: Translations

In the previous chapter, I said that there are *two* important things standing between the original writings of the Bible and us. One is the copying. The other is translating, and this chapter explains what's involved in that very important work.

The writings of the Old and New Testament authors, inspired by God, were not in our language. Without translation, the Word of God wouldn't be available to us. You and I can't help depending on translators.

Some General Truths About Translation

(1) Translating from one language into another is not a simple matter. It isn't done mechanically, one word or phrase always equal to the same word or phrase in another language. *There is no such thing as an entirely literal, word-for-word translation of the Bible that will communicate accurately.* Translation is *always* translation of *meaning*. To be sure, some translations are more literal than others, but the key to accuracy is the meaning.

(2) Consequently, translation always involves interpretation, to one degree or another. This fact applies to translation of anything. Take the famous *Iliad* by the Greek poet Homer, for example. Give that work to ten people who know Greek and English well and they will provide ten different translations. And yet, to the degree that they do their work well, all ten will say essentially what Homer said.

Sure, it is possible that in some places (especially in a long piece) the different translations will express different *meanings*, because the translators interpret the meaning differently. As I said, then, *translation*—no matter what anyone tells you—*always involves interpretation*. (That's why translators of something being spoken are called interpreters!)

Let me illustrate with some examples. First, our Spanish-speaking friends, if they want to know someone's age, may very well ask, *¿Cuantos años tiene usted?* (if they're using the polite form). If you translate this question into English "literally," you'll say, "How many years do you have?" But, since no one talks like that in English, any competent translator will say, instead, "How old are you?"—translating the meaning rather than the words.

Now that's not earth-shaking; no one minds or misunderstands the need for that. It doesn't affect the accuracy of the translation at all. But it does show that the translator has to understand—interpret—the meaning and then express that *meaning* in the translation. Often the translator can use words that correspond to the ones being translated, but sometimes he or she has to use a different form of expression. To a greater or lesser degree, *all* translation has to do that. The translator cannot avoid having to make a judgment and decide on the words to use to express the meaning.

Now an example from the New Testament. Matthew 1:18 reports that Mary "was found with child of the Holy Ghost." But that's not what the inspired, original Greek says in *words*. If you translated the *words* you would say that "she was found having in womb of (or *by*)

[the] Holy Spirit."⁵ "Having in womb," in Greek, has an obvious meaning, but no one speaking or writing English would put it that way. And the word *child* isn't in the original at all! But the obvious, correctly translated, *meaning* is that she was found to be with child.

You may respond to what I've said by saying that the Greek expression used here was one that was peculiar to them, unique in their language.⁶ That may well be true, but it remains true that the expression is not translated word for word. Furthermore, there is a great deal of the Bible that is not translated word for word in *any* of our English versions, whether our expressions parallel the original ones or not.

(3) There is often more than one way of saying the same thing in a translation. Please consider Matthew 1:18 again. There are a number of different ways a translator could say the very same thing in good, correct English:

—She was found to be with child from (or *through*) the Holy Spirit.
—She was found to be pregnant by the Holy Spirit. (We didn't use *pregnant* publicly when I was growing up!)
—It was discovered that she was expecting a baby by means of the Holy Spirit's action.
—She was found to be in a family way from the Holy Spirit.

I hope you understand that either of these (and no doubt there are others) expresses the meaning accurately. Therefore, *either of these translations is the inspired Word of God.*

You may notice that the King James says, "Holy Ghost." Given the associations of the word *ghost* these days, "Holy Spirit" is better

---
⁵The Greek is (in English letters rather than Greek characters) *heurethē en gastri echousa ek pneumatos hagiou.*
⁶The technical term for such an expression is an *idiom*. In fact, all language usage is idiomatic.

for us. By the way, have you noticed that, in the King James, "Holy Spirit" is used in some parts, while in other parts "Holy Ghost" is? That's simply because different translators were at work on the different parts! (Which tells us something about the work of translation, I think.)

All I'm saying is that words in one language can be translated more than one way and be fully accurate. Indeed, even the King James translators, in 1611, put alternate words in the margins, showing other ways of correctly translating the original.

So long as the translation of the Scriptures is accurate, so long as it communicates the right meaning, we have the original, inspired Word of God in our hands.

You will understand that I could give you *hundreds* of examples of this same principle at work.

Can Translation Be *Literal*?

Let me make another important point about translation. Yes, some translations are more "literal" than others,[7] and I like them better. But here are two things you should understand. First, a word or set of words in one language doesn't always mean *exactly* the same thing as the equivalent word or set of words in another language. No translation is completely "literal," as the example I've already given, from the King James of Matthew 1:18 shows. "Having in womb" isn't literally the same as "being with child"—even though they *mean* the same thing. Second, *being "literal" is not the most important consideration in making a translation; conveying the meaning accurately is the most important thing.* (I'll say more about preferring some translations over others in a later chapter.)

---

[7]These days, translation specialists tend to avoid using the term literal entirely, since it can be misleading. More about translation philosophy in a later chapter.

Words are funny things. Their meaning is never absolute, not handed down by some authority. They mean what people use them to mean, and the way people use them is determined by their collective and individual experiences in their own particular culture. And as time and experience go by, people use their words in growing and changing ways.

Indeed, in any language, a given word may well have a broad variety of meanings. One speaker I heard illustrated this variation in meaning, in English, with the word *trunk*, which can refer to the trunk of a car, the trunk of an elephant, or the trunk of a tree.

So, even when we think we know exactly what a Greek or Hebrew expression meant, we have to be careful. Their culture was different from ours, and there is always the chance that they didn't quite mean exactly what we mean by the best word we can use to translate.

Stay with Matthew 1:18 for an example. Mary was found "having in *womb*." But can we be sure that our word *womb* communicates *exactly* to us what the Greek word[8] meant to them? I wonder. Consider just what level of knowledge of anatomy they had in the year 4 B.C., more than two thousand years ago. Maybe some of their medical experts knew exactly what a woman's uterus is, I don't know; I'm certainly not suggesting they were completely ignorant. But I do know this: when I look up this word in my Greek dictionary, here's what I find: "*belly*," "*literally inward parts of the body, not subject to human view*." So, there isn't quite a "literal" equivalence between their word and our word *womb*, after all.

I'm not saying this inequality is a huge problem; if it were, we wouldn't be sure we can understand the Bible. And we wouldn't ever be confident we could communicate with people whose native language is different from ours. As cultures interact, the people in

---

[8]The word is *gastēr*.

one pick up on what the people in the other mean by what they say. Reading their literature contributes to that understanding. Living with them and seeing what they mean by their words helps even more. So we feel pretty confident we understand the words of the Greeks and Hebrews.

But we need to avoid being too glib about translating "literally." The work of translation isn't quite that easy.

Translation Complications

Let me illustrate the complications of translation a little more. I was recently talking with my dear brother Sherwood Lee who spent years on the mission field in West Africa and had to learn to communicate in two languages other than his native English. He reminded me that in the Lobi Bible (Lobi is a tribal language in Cote d'Ivoire, where he served) they don't translate with "heart" or "mind" when the Greek and Hebrew Bible uses those words. For *heart* they use *liver*, and for *mind* they use *stomach*. Can you love God with all your liver and with all your stomach? Well, for the Lobi, these are the seats and centers of emotions and thoughts.

Here's another example. In the Lobi Bible they don't speak "literally" about "everlasting life." They don't have that word *everlasting* in their language. So they render something like, "life for which no one knows the end." That wording is interesting, and sort of appealing.

Do these different wordings—certainly not "literal"—communicate the meaning accurately? Those who made the translation, which has been used by our missionaries in Cote d'Ivoire, were confident they understood the Lobi words well enough to believe they do. The main consideration involved in translating the Bible into Lobi—or any other language, including English—is the same: what does the original *mean*?

People who have not had much experience with other languages find it difficult to understand how translation works. What's most important, for us, is to realize that in the original writings of the inspired authors, as I said in chapter one, the very words were chosen under the supernatural, controlling inspiration of the Holy Spirit. So we have inspired words whose meanings we can figure out how to translate into our language.

Bible Translation in History: A Brief Survey

I think it will be helpful to discuss how Bible translation has developed. I won't try for a detailed history, but I will outline some of the key points that should help everyone understand how crucial the work of translation is.

The Greek Old Testament

Start with the Old Testament, even before the coming of Christ. One of the most important translations ever made was from the Hebrew-Aramaic originals into Greek, a translation called the Septuagint.[9] The name of this translation is often abbreviated with the Roman numerals for seventy—LXX—because the tradition (legendary in some ways) was that seventy (or seventy-two) Jewish scholars made this translation. It was apparently made in Alexandria in Egypt, sometime earlier than 200 B.C.

Understand: the Septuagint does not always agree, even in *meaning* (much less the words), with the Hebrew-Aramaic Old Testament. And yet a large number of the quotations from the inspired Old Testament in the inspired New Testament (some say as many as

---

[9] I am aware that the Septuagint is more a plurality of Greek translations than a single one, but for convenience I will do what most non-scholars do and refer to the whole as "the Septuagint."

two-thirds of the 300 or so such citations) *quote the Septuagint version rather than the Hebrew-Aramaic version*, even when they differ.

That fact has great importance; it means that the Holy Spirit, directing the New Testament writers in their choices of words (and we believe in plenary-verbal inspiration, remember), directed them to use a translation of the Old Testament that didn't agree in every respect with the inspired Hebrew-Aramaic. The implications of that fact are large. One of them is this: whenever the Septuagint conveys the correct meaning of the original, even though the words are different, it is the Word of God—else the New Testament writers wouldn't have quoted it as what God said.

Just so you'll know, let me give you an example. (I could give many.) In Matthew 3:3, Isaiah 40:3 is quoted and applied to John the Baptist who would cry out in the wilderness to prepare the way of the Lord and "make his paths straight." Notice the following wording of the Greek New Testament in Matthew 3:3, and of the Greek Old Testament (Septuagint) in Isaiah 40:3, and of the Hebrew text[10] (translated literally into English):

Matt. 3:3 (Greek): "make straight his paths."
Is. 40:3 (LXX): "make straight the paths of our God."
Is. 40:3 (Heb.): "make straight in the desert a path for our God."

Among the variations, notice the difference between the plural and the singular (*paths* and *path*) and the absence of "in the desert." These differences need not concern us: the essential meaning is the same. But it seems clear that Matthew is quoting the LXX translation rather than the Hebrew original.

---

[10] The basic Hebrew-Aramaic text translated into our Old Testament is what's known as the Masoretic text, having been refined by Jewish scholars in the Near East during the A.D. 600s to 900s.

I should add that there are a few places in the New Testament where it's not so clear that the Septuagint as quoted in the New Testament has exactly the same meaning as the Hebrew Old Testament. But none of these affect anything essential to Christian faith or conduct.

The point is that the inspired New Testament obviously made use of the Greek translation that didn't quite agree with the Hebrew here and there—even though it almost always agrees.

Understanding this fact helps much in understanding how different translations can still be the Word of God.

Highlights of Translation History Within the Christian Community

The history of translation is an interesting story of how God has providentially preserved His Word and ensured that it was brought to peoples all over the world in their own languages. I mention just a few key things.

(1) Early translations. Translating the Bible began early among Christians, beginning in lands not far from where the church got its start. Sometime in the third or fourth centuries (the 200s and 300s), one of the earliest was the Syriac. At about the same time, in Egypt, Coptic versions made an appearance. All of these have served the church in those areas for 1,700 years or so.

(2) The Latin Vulgate. During the period A.D. 366-384, a pious priest named Jerome translated the Bible into Latin. It came to be called the *Vulgate*, a word meaning *common*, to indicate that it was to be the common or standard version used by the Roman church. With some revisions, it has served for 1,600 years.

(3) Luther's Bible. Perhaps the single most influential thing Luther did, even more than publishing the Ninety-Five Theses, was to translate the Bible into the German language and put it in the hands

of the people. No wonder there was a "Reformation"! Most of his later years were devoted to this work. The New Testament was published in 1522 and the whole Bible in 1534. This Bible translation has put the Word of God in the hands of the Germans for almost 500 years now.

(4) Translations in other modern languages. As a result of the Reformation, the Bible was soon translated into many other languages. This process began with the languages of Europe, like French, Portuguese, Spanish, and others. The process has continued to this day, all over the world. More than 1,500 different language groups have the New Testament, and about 700 have the whole Bible. We rejoice that they have the Word of God in their hands. (Sadly, there may also be 1,500 languages where no translation is taking place.)

Translations Into English

At this point I narrow my historical survey to translations into English.

(1) Early English translations. We must realize that the English-speaking church is only a small part of the body of Christ, and the history of the Bible in our language is, by comparison, very recent.

John Wycliffe produced an English translation in 1380. He translated from the Latin Vulgate, not from the original Hebrew-Aramaic and Greek. Following the "publication" of this work (in handwritten copies), the authorities in England made it a crime, punishable by death, for anyone to possess the Scriptures in English unless licensed by the church.

(2) Translation into English really got going in the sixteenth century. In about 1525-30, translating primarily from the Latin Vulgate but making use of a few original-language manuscripts, William Tyndale produced an English version that saw widespread use. His

was the first English translation to be produced on the new printing presses, using the "movable type" invented by Gutenberg in about 1450. Tyndale himself was condemned to death for this "crime," strangled, and his body burned at the stake.

Several English translations followed soon thereafter, mostly building on the work of Tyndale. A partial list of these (there were many more) includes the Coverdale Bible (1535), Matthew's Bible (1537), the Great Bible (1540), and the Geneva Bible (1560). Those who published these were essentially improving Tyndale's translation, making more use of the materials coming available to them— like a small number of original-language manuscripts and the Greek New Testament published by Erasmus in 1516. The Geneva Bible, by the way, was apparently the one that was brought by the Pilgrims to Plymouth Rock on the Mayflower in 1620.

Many things happened to nurture this multiplication of translations in the sixteenth century: the invention of movable type that led to modern printing, the publication of Erasmus's Greek New Testament, the Church of England's break from the Roman Catholic Church in 1534 under King Henry VIII, and—last but by no means least—the public interest in the Bible that flowed from the Protestant Reformation. This period was also a time when education was becoming more public and enabling common folk to read.

(3) The King James Version (often called the *Authorized Version*) was published in 1611, produced by a group of 54 scholars appointed for that purpose by King James I of England (formerly King James VI of Scotland). As already noted, this translation—like most of the others—underwent a number of revisions; in general, what we call the King James Version (KJV) today is the revision published in 1769.

The King James translators primarily used for the Old Testament what is called the ben Hayyim edition of the ben Asher text; and for the New Testament the Greek text of Erasmus—as revised by Robert

Estienne (aka Stephanus)—and a bilingual Greek and Latin text dating to the sixth century and provided by Theodore Beza.

They also relied heavily on Tyndale's wording and that of the Geneva Bible. For the sake of illustration, I provide here a table showing the wording of these three versions in Matthew 5:1-6.

Tyndale	Geneva	King James
When he saw the people, he went up into a mountain,	And when he saw the multitude, he went up into a mountain,	And seeing the multitudes, he went up into a mountain,
and when he was set, his disciples came to him,	and when he was set, his disciples came to him	and when he was set, his disciples came unto him,
and he opened his mouth, and taught them, saying:	and he opened his mouth, and taught them, saying:	and he opened his mouth, and taught them, saying:
Blessed are the poor in spirit: for theirs is the kingdom of heaven.	Blessed are the poor in spirit: for theirs is the kingdom of heaven.	Blessed are the poor in spirit: for theirs is the kingdom of heaven.
Blessed are they that mourn: for they shall be comforted.	Blessed are they that mourn: for they shall be comforted.	Blessed are they that mourn: for they shall be comforted.
Blessed are the meek: for they shall inherit the earth.	Blessed are the meek: for they shall inherit the earth.	Blessed are the meek: for they shall inherit the earth.
Blessed are they which hunger and thirst for righteousness: for they shall be filled.	Blessed are they which hunger and thirst for righteousness for they shall be filled.	Blessed are they which do hunger and thirst after righteousness: for they shall be filled.

Several things seem obvious. (1) There is no real difference in meaning here. (2) The King James translators were not striving for "new" wording; indeed, in their very lengthy and significant preface to the 1611 version they said they were not producing a new translation but trying to make a good one better. I will provide a chapter later giving excerpts from the preface to the King James. (Anyone interested in this subject should get a copy and read the whole preface; it is available online.) (3) There is every reason to regard all three as the Word of God.

(4) Modern English versions. After the King James Version went through various revisions, that same process led to more complete revisions in modern versions. First was the English Revised Version, in 1885 in Great Britain, followed by its American counterpart, the American Standard Version, in 1901. Among some of the more well-known versions since then are the Revised Standard Version (RSV, 1952), the New American Standard Bible (NASB, 1960), the New International Version (NIV, 1978), and the English Standard Version (ESV, 2001). There are, indeed, too many to name. (I will have more to say about English versions in a later chapter.)

Different Translators and the Word of God

From this brief rehearsal of the history of translating the Scriptures, the following ought to be clear. Thousands of translators, during the past 2,000 years, have worked to translate into the languages of mankind the inspired Word of God. While it is obvious to all that translators do their work as humans and are not inspired, it is also obvious that we have the inspired originals to check their work by. We have enough devout servants of the Lord involved in doing this work that we can be sure when a translation accurately conveys the meaning of the original. And so we can be sure that we have the Word of God in our hands. Translation is one of the ways God has preserved His Word.

Our confidence in the Bible as the Word of God is not based on the character and beliefs of the translators. They have represented all strands of Christianity, broadly conceived: Calvinists and Arminians; Baptists, Methodists, Presbyterians, and Pentecostals; and people with wide differences in how they practice their faith. (Only a couple that I know have been part of our denomination: Lonnie Sparks in Cote d'Ivoire producing the Kulango New Testament, and Bill Jones in the same country contributing to the Agni translation. I wish there had been more of us!)

There's simply no reason to believe that all or any of these folks were divinely inspired or miraculously caused to do perfect work that can never be improved.

It seems obvious that this applies to the King James translators as much as to any others. We have to be wise, here: *there is no version or translation anywhere in the world that is like the King James, word for word.* There is no reason there should be, or that we should judge other versions by how closely they match the King James. *It doesn't make sense to take a view of translation that applies only in the English language.*

In other words we can only judge the value of a translation by one standard: namely, how accurately it conveys the meaning of the original.

This standard, of course, raises a question: if you don't know Greek and Hebrew well, how can you judge how well a translation conveys the meaning of the original? The answer is that you have to be discerning. Compare versions for accuracy. Make sure about those whom you trust to do such evaluating. I will return to this matter in a later chapter.

Who Has the Word of God?

Given the huge variety of translations into various languages, then, we need to think about this question. The answer, in a nutshell, is this: Anyone who has a Bible that accurately conveys the meaning of the original, in his or her language, has the Word of God. I don't see that any other answer is possible.

That means, then, that the early church had the Word of God. So did the developing church—those in the West who depended on the Latin as well as those in the East who depended on the Greek. So did Christian heroes like Augustine and Luther and Tyndale. So do people in a thousand modern language groups and those who use modern English versions that accurately convey the meaning of the original. We don't need to think we're the only ones who have the Word of God; indeed, such a way of thinking would be dramatically hostile to the work of God in preserving His Word in the world.

Indeed, I'm going to risk something here and say this: even those English-speaking people who had a copy of "the Wicked Bible," which said "Thou shalt commit adultery," had the Word of God in their hands and rejoiced in it. How can I say such a thing? Well, of course that particular sentence, as published, wasn't the Word of God. But those who had that Bible recognized the typesetter's error and understood that their Bibles *as a whole* were the Word of God.

When human beings make mistakes with the things of God, that doesn't change the things of God. Especially when the mistake is readily recognized. Anyone reading the "Wicked Bible" knew that omitting the "not" was a human error, and that God's Word remained established and known in spite of human error.

One of the things involved in this matter is realizing that all the things that have transpired in bringing the Word of God to us have transpired *in the providence of God*. That includes the mistakes humans make, the differences in the manuscripts, and the great variety of translations. I don't mean, of course, that God has caused the mistakes to be made, or that He approves of every manuscript or translation. I won't take space here to discuss how God's providence is at work in all the variety, but I will devote much of a chapter to the providence of God later in this volume.

In His providence, God has preserved His Word in the world. And wherever there are any differences in our Bibles we human beings must and can discern just which of the differences represents the Word He has preserved. That is our confidence, and that is our responsibility.

Am I saying that God's preservation of His Word makes everything wonderful and that there's no need for careful judgment about versions? No, as I will make clear in a chapter to come. The providence of God at work in all our circumstances doesn't prevent us from mistakes. It doesn't free us from the threat of falsehood that will condemn us if we are not spiritually perceptive. We have to be discerning, not naïve.

All of what I've said about God's providence applies to the way the Word of God has been preserved and brought to us. For the most part, the human beings doing the work of copying and translating have been careful to do it right. They have exercised great human effort—often very meticulous and rigorous effort—to try to make sure the manuscripts were copied accurately, and to translate the meaning of the originals into the languages of people in such a way that they know what God has said to them.

But—yes, in God's providence—that carefulness did not keep differences in the manuscripts and the translations from appearing. Again, human beings were at work as human beings. Differences should surprise no one. But, by and large, the same kind of human beings as those who did this work can figure out just which ones got it right. And where there are a few differences, about which one cannot be 100% sure, we rejoice to know that not a single item of doctrine we are meant to believe is at stake. And not a single item of what we are meant to practice is at stake.

People may magnify those differences if they wish. But when they do, they are missing the joy of knowing that God has providentially preserved His Word for us in the human work of scribes and translators—not to mention those who preach and teach to make sure the meaning of the Book is clear, as imperfectly as they do their ministry.

Conclusion

In conclusion to these last two chapters, I hope you will keep in mind that there have been thousands of copyists and translators who stand between us and the original writings of the "holy men" who were "borne along by the Holy Spirit." These latter were the ones who were, indeed, miraculously preserved from all error.

What then about the scribes and translators who were (and are) involved in bringing the Word of God to us? They are *human beings doing human work* with the Word of God entrusted to us. Miracles were not being performed by those copyists and translators, regardless what manuscripts or versions they worked to produce.

We should understand that they have been working for God in the very same way that Christian ministers of the gospel, missionaries, evangelists, Bible teachers, theologians, and Bible scholars work for God, and under the very same influences.

Except for special circumstances like the inspiration of the original writers of the Scripture, God always works through fallible human beings to do His work. In His providence, He uses them to accomplish His purposes. They aren't perfect; they sometimes make mistakes. But God brings His truth to light and preserves it in spite of that.

In the case of the Bible, He has providentially preserved His Word in the work of all these thousands of scribes and translators.

I know there is yet much to be said, and I'll try to say it in subsequent chapters. Meanwhile, you should know that in spite of the human fallibility of the scribes and translators we know what God's Word is. Our Bibles are the Word of God. And I repeat something important that I said already: none of the differences in manuscripts and translations prevent us from knowing what God has said to us. There is not a single matter of Christian doctrine or practice that is at stake in these differences.

CHAPTER FOUR
The Bible in the Language of the People: The Original Text and the Goal of Translations

The Bible ought to be in the language of the people who need to know what God has said to them. That much is obvious. After all, God has spoken to us in the Bible. Second Timothy 3:16, as we have noticed, says that all Scripture is God-breathed. It has been given to us by inspiration, as I've discussed in chapter one.

But that's not all the verse says. Immediately comes this addition: "and is profitable for doctrine, for reproof, for correction, for instruction in righteousness" (that is, in right living). The Bible was meant to tell us things, to communicate to us and make a difference in our beliefs and behavior. It can't do that unless it is in the language we use and understand.

The Bible as God's Revealing Himself to Us

In the Bible, God *reveals* Himself and the truth we need to know about ourselves and the provision He has made for our redemption. But in order to reveal anything to us, it must speak to us in words we understand.

Some philosophers question whether an infinite God, in His transcendence—which means His apartness from and unlikeness to us—can communicate with finite human beings who are so different from Him that they cannot possibly understand or know Him. I won't take time to explore that issue, saying only that it is a foolish question. In light of the fact that God made us in His likeness and knows us perfectly, He can communicate with us in all our languages. Ever since creation, God has been speaking to human beings, and the Bible provides the story of that communication. Indeed, in one sense it *is* that communication.

He who knows our thoughts and words is certainly capable of understanding what we say and of using our admittedly limited languages as a means of communicating with us. We certainly cannot know *everything* there is to know about God, but we can know what He chooses to reveal about Himself. We can't know Him exhaustively, but we can know correctly what He enables us to know. And when He guided the writing prophets and apostles to speak to us, He chose to reveal Himself.

If we could not understand what He said in the Bible, then it would reveal nothing to us. We would not know about our lostness or about the provision He has made for us to know Him and be saved.

When the Church Allowed the Bible to Be Hidden

As obvious as our need for the Bible is to us, the church has not always understood it. As the Roman church developed its traditions, its extra-biblical doctrines, its hierarchical structure, and its priestly clergy, it also moved out well beyond its original centers into all of Europe. The Latin language, which had been the language of the people in Rome, say, was no longer the language of many of those under the influence of the church. But Latin remained the language of the clergy—and of the Bible.

As early church history moved into the Middle Ages, the Bible ceased to be available to most of the people, the laity. That didn't really matter to the clergy. The less the laity knew about the Bible, the more they depended on the clergy to tell them what it said and what it meant. The clergy were happy to instruct the laity as they wanted them instructed. They went along undisturbed, speaking Latin to people who didn't understand it, keeping the Latin Bible to themselves. Ultimately they discouraged—or even forbade—the laity from having Bibles of their own. And that was not difficult to enforce since the only Bibles available were expensive, hand-made copies in Latin.

That is a bleak picture indeed—and one I have painted only in broad strokes, making no effort to provide historical detail. The separation of the people from the Word of God is what matters, and it was very real.

I should add that the Medieval Church, in allowing this separation to happen, had strayed far from what Christianity had originally understood well: namely, that the Word of God was intended to be in the hands of the people.

The Effects of the Reformation

The Reformation changed all that. The Reformers wanted the common folk to have and read the Bible for themselves. And the invention of printing presses that used movable type helped make that possible. I have already mentioned that one of Luther's greatest contributions to the body of Christ was translating the Bible into German.

That made it possible, for the first time, for the ordinary German Christians to own and read the Word of God.

The Reformation emphasized, among other things, the priesthood of every believer. That means no one else stands between us in our relationship with God. All of us are priests in the sense that we can approach God directly. We can and should read His Word for ourselves and in that way hear what He has to say to us.

Our priesthood means that each of us is free, and responsible, to interpret the Word, to discern its principles and conscientiously apply those principles in our daily lives. Each of us is answerable to God for what He has said and what it means in our faith and conduct. Although we don't become independent of the church, we also don't bow to the dominion of clergy as though they mediate God's presence to us. We come straight to God.

I could continue along these lines at length but won't, lest the main point be lost sight of. That point is this: for us to hear what God says He must speak to us in the language we use and understand well. And so the Bible must be in our hands and in our languages.

Some History of the Bible

Let's put this truth in the context of the history of the Bible. Consider the Old Testament, written mostly in Hebrew with a small part in Aramaic. When Moses and Isaiah and the others were inspired as "holy men of old" to write what God intended to be His Word, they wrote for the people of their time, ancient Israel. During much of Old Testament history their language was Hebrew, the very language that most of the Old Testament is in. And it was apparently not some "special" brand or dialect of Hebrew, it was the Hebrew used and understood by the people.

Later, especially during and following the Babylonian captivity, many in Israel began to use Aramaic instead of Hebrew. Aramaic (see 2 Kings 18:26, "the Syrian language") had become the common language of much of the Near East. So parts of the original Daniel and Ezra, in the Bible, are in Aramaic. The language of these parts, too, was apparently the language of everyday life among them at that time. They could use and understand it.

The Nature of New Testament Greek

I can speak even more confidently about the Greek of the New Testament, and understanding this language makes for an interesting story. Until the nineteenth century, say, students of the Greek of the New Testament had access, other than the New Testament itself, only to classical Greek documents and some later, literary Greek. The problem was that the Greek of the New Testament—in vocabulary and grammar—was significantly different from classical and literary Greek. So for a long time some thought that the Greek of the New Testament was perhaps a special, "Holy Ghost" kind of usage, unlike regular Greek because it was inspired.

But then came the discovery of thousands of Greek writings from the very same period of time as the New Testament. Many of these were on papyrus and many had been preserved in the tombs and dry climate of Egypt—although there are also some from other places. And these were things written by ordinary people, things like letters to one's family. As more and more of these were brought to light and read by the scholars they began to realize that they were looking at the Greek language *as it was used in everyday life by ordinary people at the same time as when the New Testament was written.*

And, even more important, they soon realized that the language of these documents was the very same language—vocabulary and structure—as the Greek of the New Testament. This was a stunning realization, and it changed the way the language of the New Testament was viewed—not to mention the understanding of a lot of its words and ideas. And many of these discoveries and realizations did not take place until the nineteenth century, long after the early English translations were published.

The point of what I've said is clear: the Greek New Testament was written in the kind of Greek that common, everyday people used in their ordinary affairs.[11] The technical term for the everyday language of people, in any language—as compared, say, to a more *literary* usage—is the *vernacular*. The New Testament, in the original Greek, is in the vernacular of its time, inspired that way by God. (But I'll continue to refer to this as the everyday language of ordinary folks.)

One of the leading scholars in coming to this realization was Adolf Deissmann (1866-1937), and his book that made the headlines in demonstrating the nature of New Testament Greek was *Light from the Ancient East*, published in 1908 (English translation in 1910). Please take note of the fact that this was 300 years and more *after* that period when the early English versions, including the King James, were published in the sixteenth and seventeenth centuries. That fact has important implications, since the later discoveries shed much light on the meaning of the Greek in the New Testament.

As a result of those discoveries and the conclusions to which they led, the Greek of the New Testament came to be known as *Koine* (pronounce it *coin-ā*) Greek, and the period during which the New Testament was written is called the *Koine* period. *Koine* means "common," and the Greek of that time is called by this name because it was the common language of people of the time. Indeed, the usage of Greek had spread widely and was the common language of a large part of the Roman Empire during the time of the New Testament.

To sum up, God gave us His word in the very language that Greek-speaking people used and understood. He gave it to them not

---

[11]There is a danger that I am too simplistic here. Different writers of the Greek New Testament exhibited different styles and levels of usage. Luke's usage, for example, is of a higher and more complex style than that of John. But all used the language as it would have been readily understood by their first readers.

in some special or elevated form of their language, but in the same way they used it in communicating with each other in their everyday world.

How wonderful and compassionate of our God! And how like Him that is! He spoke to human beings in the very language they used and understood. How else could He have communicated to us so fully and effectively?

Getting the Bible to People in Their Languages

Once the church got the idea that God intended for His Word to be in the language of ordinary people, the work of getting God's Word to people in their languages became a high priority. Starting with Luther's translation into German, the new impetus led to translations in many languages, first in Europe and ultimately everywhere else. Luther wanted the German peasants to be able to read what God had spoken. French-speaking leaders wanted that for French believers. And so did countless others, from then until now.

I have written about this history briefly in the previous chapter and need not repeat. All Christians, I think, realize the importance of having the Word of God available to people anywhere, regardless what language they speak, in what some call their "heart language." This expression means the language in which people were born, the language of their own particular culture. It is the language in which they have grown up, the one they understand best, the one whose words and expressions speak most directly to them.

This need, to hear God speak in one's native tongue, is the reason people devote themselves to special education in linguistic skills, to lonely years in a foreign land, learning a given people's language by living among them, to reducing that language to writing, and then to translating (from the Hebrew/Aramaic and Greek originals) into the language of people who have not had direct access to God's written

Word. To meet this need, organizations like Wycliffe Bible Translators exist, to make the Bible available to people who haven't had access to it before.

Ultimately, knowing God depends on knowing His word. And people cannot hear God's word unless it is expressed in the language they use and understand.

The Bible in English: The King James Version

Everything I've been saying to this point applies in the very same way to us for whom English is our heart language. If the Bible is not translated into our language, the very way we use and understand it, we might not hear what He said at all or might misunderstand it—at risk of our souls.

Indeed, that is exactly what the King James translators believed and intended: to provide English-speaking people the Word of God in the everyday language they used and understood. That is essentially what they said they were doing in the preface to the King James, and I will share important excerpts from that preface with you in a later chapter. Just as the Greek New Testament was in the everyday language of the people who first read it, so the King James was in the everyday English of those who first read it.

True, there are words in the King James that *we* do not understand, but that's not the fault of the King James translators. It's because the language has changed. I'll expand on this change in the next chapter. But the people for whom it was first published understood the words very well, because they were the words they themselves used.

That is also true for the Elizabethan pronoun forms—like *thou*, *thee*, and *ye*—and the strange verb endings—like *eth*, *est*, etc.—that went with them. They were not strange to the ears of the people of England in 1611.

In the next chapter, I will provide a very brief survey of the history of the English language and give some additional attention to these pronouns and the strange verb forms used with them. For now, however, I want to emphasize that they were used and understood by the people of England at that time. Shakespeare, writing at about the same time, used them also.

Sometimes people make a mistake, understandable enough, in thinking that these pronouns expressed a special respect for people or for God. All one has to do to correct this misunderstanding is read the King James carefully, paying attention to the pronouns and these verb endings. If you do this, you will immediately realize that *thou* is used for *anyone*, whether God or ruler or common person. To a leper in Mark 1:41, 44 Jesus said "Be thou clean" and "Shew thyself to the priest." Lepers were shunned by all, the very opposite of anyone special.

Both in the original Greek (the Hebrew Old Testament too) and in the King James English, *the very same pronouns and verb endings were used for addressing ordinary human beings as were used for addressing God.* And that is just one small illustration of a very large and important fact: namely, that there is nothing special about the languages—Hebrew, Aramaic, and Greek—used in the Bible. Those languages, like hundreds of others, are simply the languages of ordinary human beings.

What I've said is true in the very same way for the English of the King James. Clearly, our God wanted His word to be expressed to us in our language and in the very way we use and understand it—not in some special or quaint or even "majestic" way.

There is no reason for us to make a translation, in English, that uses language in any way different from the way God Himself used the Greek of the New Testament. He used Greek just as Greek-speaking people used it at the time. That must be the best way to use language for the Word of God. That's the way English should be used in expressing the Word of God, and that's exactly the way it was used in making the King James Version. That's the way any language should be used when translating the Word of God. That's what translation is about.

To say this another way, the inspired New Testament is in the ordinary Greek of its time. The King James Version is in the ordinary English of its time. It's easy to see, then, why many believe that the Bible should be in the ordinary English of *our* time. Indeed, shouldn't all people everywhere be able to read the Word of God in their language as they naturally use and understand it?

For an illustration to close this chapter, I want to provide an example, not from the Bible itself, of how the English language was used at the same time the King James was translated. Indeed, this example shows how the very same people used it, since it is a brief excerpt from the preface to the King James.

I've already said that I will devote a later chapter in this book to the original preface to the King James. There I will focus on *what* they said. Here, however, I ask you to focus on *how* they said it. This excerpt will help you see how much difference there is between the English of 1611 and the English of today.

The Perfections of the Scriptures

But now what piety without truth? What truth, what saving truth, without the word of God? What word of God, whereof we may be sure, without the Scriptures? ... In a word, it [the Scripture] is a panary of wholesome food against fenowed traditions; a physician's shop ... of preservatives against poisoned heresies; a pandect of profitable laws against rebellious spirits; a treasure of most costly jewels against beggarly rudiments; finally, a fountain of most pure water springing up unto everlasting life. And what marvel? The original thereof being from heaven, not from earth;

the author being God, not man; the inditer, the Holy Spirit, not the wit of the Apostles or Prophets; the penmen, such as were sanctified from the womb, and endued with a principal portion of God's Spirit.

In case you're wondering, *panary* means a bread-supply, *fenowned* means moldy, a *pandect* is a code of laws, and an *inditer* is a composer.

CHAPTER FIVE
What You Need to Know About the English of the King James

As I've said before, my purpose is not to persuade people to use some version other than the King James. And it certainly isn't to criticize the King James.

But anyone who is interested in the subject of this book needs to understand some things about the English of the King James. A wise person wants to know everything that's involved in an issue.

And a good understanding of the King James English is not nearly so prevalent as many people think. My purpose here is to contribute to such an understanding.

Background: Some History of the English Language

All human languages change over time, which means that an accurate translation needs to be faithful both to the original language and to the language of the translation at any given time in history. Such change is inevitable, resulting from growing experience, changing culture, and interaction with other peoples. This fact of change is just as true of English as it is of any other language. Consequently, a brief survey of the history of the English language should be helpful in giving readers a better grasp of everything I will say.

Historians of our language usually divide the discussion into three broad periods of time.[12]

First was "Old English," from about A.D. 450 to 1100. This period began when some mostly Germanic tribes (Angles, Saxons, Jutes) from Europe migrated to the British Isles and gradually mingled their dialects, producing what some call Anglo-Saxon, the original form of the English language.

Probably the most well-known writing from this Old English period is an anonymous, lengthy (3,183 lines!), epic poem named "Beowulf." Only specialists can read it in its original form. The opening lines go something like this (I say "something" since there are a couple of characters that don't quite match our letters):

> *HWÄT! We Gâr-Dena in gear-dagum peód-cybinga prym gefrunon, pâ ädelingas ellen fremedon.*

I certainly don't know what these lines say, *but the language is English.* (And the last two words are *not* the name of a person named Ellen Fremedon!)

The *second* period was "Middle English," from about 1100 to 1500. This period began when the Duke of Normandy conquered England. French (for the ruling class) and Latin (for the church, especially) became widely used (and affected English), and English became the language of the lower classes.

Perhaps the most well-known piece of literature from this period was Chaucer's *Canterbury Tales*, written during the period 1387-1400, which begins thus:

> *Whan that Aprill with his shoures soote*
> *The droghte of March hath perced to the roote . . .*

---

[12]For the following, I have used "A Brief History of the English Language," accessed at www.studyenglishtoday.net/english-language-history.htm.

With a little work and help, a modern reader can figure these lines out. But the difference between English then and English now is still quite large.

Third was "Modern English," from about 1500 to the present. The beginning of this period was marked by the establishment of the first printing press in England in about 1476. In many ways the invention of printing served to standardize the language, although it continued to develop as the English culture developed, especially by the adoption of many words from other languages. The Industrial Revolution and England's aggressive, world-wide colonization also contributed to the changes.

Earlier, I indicated that a number of English translations of the Bible were published in the 1500s and early 1600s, including that of William Tyndale in 1525-30 and the King James, first published in 1611. These appeared during the "Early Modern" period (1500s and 1600s), also known as the age of Shakespeare or the Elizabethan era, reflecting its most prominent writer and famous, long-reigning queen.

In many ways, the English usage of the King James is like that of Shakespeare. Both were written as the language actually existed and would be understood during that period. And both are different in significant ways from the language as it exists and is understood now.

An Ever-Changing Language

The English language continues to change. For that matter, the English used in England and the English used in America have developed in somewhat different ways, and not just in pronunciation.

It is true, of course, that people still read the King James—and Shakespeare—and understand it. For the most part, however, these are people who have a church background, who have grown up reading the King James or hearing it read, or have been exposed to Shakespeare in their education.

But people who have not had these advantages find the language of Shakespeare and the King James Version difficult, if not remote. The King James is not in the language of their lives. They struggle to understand some of it.

The Strange Pronouns and Verb Endings

One of the things that makes the King James difficult, or at least strange, is the pronouns—specifically second person singular and plural—and the unique verb endings that go with them (and in third person singular constructions). As the subject of a sentence, the second singular pronoun is *thou*, as an object it is *thee*, and the possessive forms are *thy* and *thine*. The corresponding plural forms are *ye*, *you*, and *your*. The difference in these meant that you could always tell whether one person or more than one was meant. Our current English usage has lost this feature, and this loss is something of a disadvantage. We have to depend on context to know whether *you* is singular or plural.

The verb endings that went with *thou* are also strange to us. So we read sentences like this: "And he said, Who told thee that thou wast naked? Hast thou eaten of the tree, whereof I commanded thee that thou shouldest not eat?" (Gen. 3:11). There are many sentences like this one in the King James, and many current readers find these off-putting.

Words Whose Meanings Have Changed

More important than the Elizabethan pronouns and verb endings is the fact that the meaning of words has changed since 1611 when the King James was published. Many people realize this fact, of course, but not many realize how extensive (and sometimes subtle) these changes are.

I will devote the rest of this chapter to the changes in the meanings of words between the time of the King James and the present. For convenience and better understanding, I will present these changes in two groups and I will illustrate them at considerable length.[13] It is important that readers understand just how extensive these changes are.

In other words, in some ways the King James translation needs to be translated! And, by the way, there are some dictionaries of King James words for this very purpose.[14]

I. Words That Are no Longer Used at All or With the Same Meaning as in the King James

There are many words used in the King James that are no longer used in the English language or, if they are still used, have a very different meaning from what they meant in 1611. These changes mean, simply, that there are a lot of English-speaking people who will not understand the meaning of these words correctly unless they obtain extra help.

I have selected fifteen of these as illustrations, appearing here in alphabetical order. There could be many more, but these are enough to show both that such words occur and that they are more numerous than many think. Most of these words (or at least the meanings they have in the King James) will be marked in a good dictionary as *Obsolete* (no longer in usage) or *Archaic* (belonging to an earlier usage, not current).

---

[13]For suggestions about some of these words, not all of them, I have consulted some lists made by others, both in books and in online resources. But the treatment I give them is my own.

[14]There are some dictionaries of King James words online, and they are very helpful for understanding the Bible.

(1) *Bewray*. Here's a word that's no longer used at all. It looks enough like *betray* that we may think it means that.

Isa. 16:3: "*Bewray* not him that wandereth."

Prov. 27:16: "Whosoever hideth her hideth ...the ointment of his right hand, which *bewrayeth* itself."

Prov. 29:24: "He heareth cursing, and *bewrayeth* it not."

For those who read the King James in 1611, the word meant to expose or reveal. Thus, people who *think* it means to betray won't miss it too far—as in Matthew 26:73, "Thy speech bewrayeth thee"—but in fact the word doesn't carry the notion of betrayal.

(2) *Bray*. To us, this word refers to the loud, harsh sound a donkey makes—and this meaning *is* found in the Bible, as in Job 6:5: "Doth the wild ass bray when he hath grass?" But what about the following?

Prov. 27:22: "Though thou shouldest *bray* a fool in a mortar among wheat with a pestle, yet will not his foolishness depart from him."

In this verse, *bray* means to crush or pound to a powder.

(3) *Bruit*. In English usage these days, this archaic word doesn't mean much at all. In 1611 it meant a noise, uproar, clamor, rumor, or report.

Jer. 10:22: "Behold, the noise of the *bruit* is come." (Try "rumor" or "report.")

Nah. 3:19: "All that hear the *bruit* of thee shall clap the hands over thee." (Try "report" or "news.")

(4) *Chambering*. Today, as a verb, *chamber* means either to provide a chamber or compartment for some use, or to put something in a chamber—like cartridges into a gun. Such a meaning won't fit the following—which, I think, is the only time the word is used as a verb in the Bible.

Rom. 13:13: "Let us walk honestly ... not in *chambering* and wantonness."

It's another word for sexual immorality, perhaps conceiving such immorality as "bedrooming"—much like we speak of "going to bed" with someone. Some modern readers might guess that, of course, but most probably will not.

(5) *Communicate.* For us, this word usually means to give information or express something to another person. That doesn't work well in the King James.

> Gal. 6:6: "Let him that is taught in the word *communicate* unto him that teacheth in all good things."
>
> Phil. 4:15: "No church *communicated* with me, as concerning giving and receiving, but ye only."

In 1611 this word meant to share with someone, and in this context the Word means that those who are taught the things of God are obligated to share "all good things" with their teachers in order to support their teaching ministry. The Philippian church had done just that for Paul, their teacher.

(6) *Hale.* This is an adjective that now means physically sound, healthy—as in the expression "hale and hearty." Will that meaning work in the following?

> Lk. 12:58: "Lest he *hale* thee to the judge."

Our contemporary meaning won't work. In the King James this word is a verb, and it meant to drag or haul. Jesus was saying we should take measures to avoid being hauled into court.

(7) *Leasing.* To us, this word means something like a long-term or formal rental. If you assume that meaning in the following, you won't hear what God's Word says.

> Psa. 4:2: "How long will ye love vanity, and seek after *leasing?*"
>
> Psa. 5:6: "Thou shalt destroy them that speak *leasing.*"

In the King James, this word means falsehood or lying.

(8) *Let.* For us this word means to permit or allow (if not to rent out or lease!). It also means this *sometimes* in the Bible. But that meaning won't work in the following verses.

2 Thess. 2:7: "He who now *letteth* will *let*, until he be taken out of the way."

Rom. 1:13: "Oftentimes I purposed to come unto you, (but was *let* hitherto)."

In 1611, one of the meanings of *let* was to hinder, hold back, restrain. In Thessalonians there is something ("what," v. 6) or someone ("who," v. 7) holding back the full manifestation of the "man of sin." And Paul had often made plans to go to Rome but had been hindered in that purpose.

(9) *Prevent.* In today's English, this verb means to hinder or stop something from happening. But that meaning doesn't always work in King James usage.

1 Thess. 4:15: "We which are alive and remain ... shall not *prevent* them which are asleep."

Matt. 17:25: "When he was come into the house, Jesus *prevented* him [Peter]."

Psa. 21:3: "Thou *preventest* him with the blessings of goodness."

When the King James was translated, this verb meant to anticipate or precede. Living believers will not *precede* or get ahead of the dead in Christ when He returns. Jesus *anticipated* Simon with His question, speaking first. David senses that the Lord is *out ahead of him* in the blessings received. (These are just three of many where lots of people miss the meaning.)

(10) *Reins.* These days, this noun usually refers to a pair of lines used to guide or check a horse or mule. Will that meaning help one understand these?

Psa. 139:13: "Thou hast possessed my *reins.*"

Psa. 16:7: "My *reins* also instruct me in the night seasons."

Prov. 23:16: "My *reins* shall rejoice when thy lips speak right things."

In 1611, this noun referred to one's *kidneys*. But the true meaning was yet another layer of language and culture deeper than that, indicating the seat of one's affections in the inner being. Today, we use a word like *heart*. God isn't guiding us like we guide horses, but He does speak to us in our innermost being. (I have actually heard one of our preachers preach that in a certain passage the reins indicated that God guides us, as we do a horse, by pulling on the reins!)

I'm aware that this word can still mean *kidneys*, in the medical profession at least, where the same root shows up in the phrase *renal disease*. But who knew that?

(11) *Scrip*. I'm not sure what this archaic word might mean in today's English usage. It can refer to a piece of paper with something written on it, like a certificate of indebtedness or paper money. That certainly isn't the meaning in the King James.

Matt. 10:10: "Nor *scrip* for your journey."

1 Sam. 17:40: "He took ... five smooth stones ... and put them in a shepherd's bag ...even in a *scrip*."

At the time, the word meant something like a wallet or small bag, often used by shepherds or travelers—we might say a *purse*. When Jesus sent out the twelve on this mission, they were not to take provisions but depend on those to whom they would minister. David used his for the stones he would sling at Goliath, and a person reading this passage would probably figure out what it meant since it is equated to a shepherd's bag. But in the Gospels, it isn't a *shepherd's* bag.

(12) *Shambles*. In today's English, this word is most likely to refer to a scene where there is great destruction or disorder. That isn't the meaning in the Bible.

1 Cor. 10:25: "Whatever is sold in the *shambles*, that eat."

Anyone reading this verse would probably discern that "the shambles" was a place where something could be sold and bought. It actually means a slaughterhouse (which could suggest the source of our modern use of the word) or meat market. (Some Brits still use it in the latter sense.)

(13) *Sod*. In our usage, sod is a layer of earth with the grass in it. But that's an entirely different word from the following.

Gen. 25:29: "And Jacob *sod* pottage."

2 Chron. 35:13: "The other holy offerings *sod* they in pots."

Try *boiled* for these and you'll have the right meaning. (And what in the world is *pottage*? Jacob was cooking soup or stew.) Actually *sod* is the past of *seethe*, as in Exod. 23:19: "Thou shalt not *seethe* a kid in his mother's milk." And *sodden* is the past participle, as in Lam. 4:10: "The hands of the pitiful women have *sodden* their own children." (Our modern usage of *sodden* to mean *soaked* is closely related.)

(14) *Trow*. We just don't use this archaic word any more with *any* meaning. So what does it mean in the King James?

Lk. 17:9: "Doth he thank that servant...? I *trow* not."

While today's readers may get the right idea here, the chances are they won't get the exact meaning. *Trow* meant, in 1611, to believe, think, suppose, reckon.

(15) *Wot*. Here's another archaic word we don't use at all. For the following, then, we may figure out the meaning in context, but our own present usage provides no clue to its meaning.

Acts 3:17: "I *wot* that through ignorance ye did it."

Gen. 39:8: "My master *wotteth* not what is with me."

Phil. 1:22: "What I shall choose I *wot* not."

In the King James, this old verb means to know or learn. It is an interesting verb, by the way, and the root (infinitive) form is *wit*: I wot; thou wost/wottest; he wot/wotteth; we or ye or they wite/witen.

Consider also 2 Cor. 8:1: "We do you to *wit* of the grace of God." "We do you to wit of" simply means (as the Greek original says), "We make known to you."

II. Words That May (Mistakenly) Seem to Mean the Same Thing Now but Really Don't

In some ways, these words create more of a problem for readers than the ones above. Most English readers, today, when they encounter the words in the list above, will recognize that they don't know what they mean and will make an effort to find out what they meant when the King James was published. But the words in this list tend to fool us into thinking we know what they mean when we don't. One writer I know about calls these "false friends."[15]

When we see these words, we immediately recognize them and have meanings for them in our minds. Those meanings *seem* to fit the text and we go on, never suspecting that we didn't quite get it right. The point is that there have been changes in English usage during the four hundred years since the King James was published. And some of those changes are subtle ones, changes many people are unaware of. What the words convey to us today isn't quite what they conveyed to readers in 1611.

I am going to list another fifteen examples, again in alphabetical order. As with the list above, there could be many more. These should be enough to make readers aware of the danger of taking all the words in the King James Bible to mean what they *seem* to mean. The precise meaning of the Word of God is at stake here.

(1) *Careful*. When people are careful, that means they proceed with caution or do their work painstakingly or thoughtfully, or something like that—which is a good thing. But Paul advises against it!

Phil. 4:6: "Be *careful* for nothing."

Surely he didn't mean that! Yes, he did: this word had a different meaning in 1611. It meant the same as our *worried* or *anxious*—and

---

[15]Mark Ward, *Authorized: The Use and Misuse of the King James Bible* (Bellingham, WA: Lexham Press, 2018).

so Paul's prohibition fits right in with what Jesus said in Matthew 6:25, where the Greek word is the same as here. Jesus' rebuke to Martha in Luke 10:41 (where the same word occurs again) is also correctly understood in this light.

(2) *Carriage(s)*. Here's a word with some different meanings in current English usage, like a four-wheeled horse-drawn vehicle or a baby carriage. None of the meanings we have fit the King James usage.

>Acts 21:15: "We took up our *carriages*, and went up to Jerusalem."

>1 Sam. 17:22: "And David left his *carriage* in the hand of the keeper of the *carriage*."

It isn't hard to guess at the meaning. *Carriage* is something one carries. When the word appears in the King James it means something like what we call baggage or luggage.

(3) *Closet*. If we refer to a closet these days, the chances are we mean a relatively small room where we hang our clothes or store other things. That is not the way we should read the following.

>Matt. 6:6: "When thou prayest, enter into thy *closet*."

In spite of the fact that we often hear reference to a "prayer closet," *closet* does not mean what it seems to mean. When the King James was published, a closet was simply a closed-off place, like a room where one could shut the door and be alone. Any room could be a closet. Consider also:

>Joel 2:16: "Let the bridegroom go forth of his chamber, and the bride out of her *closet*."

>Lk. 12:3: "That which ye have spoken ... in *closets* shall be proclaimed upon the housetops."

Don't think of any of these as being like our modern closets.

(4) *Coast(s)*. As a noun in current English usage, this one means land alongside a body of water. That is not what it meant in the King James usage.

Matt. 16:13: "Jesus came into the *coasts* of Caesarea Philippi."

Matt. 8:34: "They besought him that he would depart out of their *coasts*."

In such places (and this word occurs many times in the Bible) the word means, simply, the border or the territory or region within the borders.

It would be especially tempting, in Acts 27:2, where Paul's company were "meaning to sail by the coasts of Asia" and the sea is involved, to think that *coasts* meant what it does in our current usage. But it probably meant only the territory of (the Roman province of) Asia; the Greek simply says "the *places*" in (that is, along the boundaries of) Asia.

(5) *Convenient*. For us, this word means that something is easy to access or use, handy, not a bother or trouble. What about in the following?

Eph. 5:4: "Neither filthiness, nor foolish talking, nor jesting, which are not *convenient*."

Try as we might, we can't quite fit the meaning we associate with this word into Paul's prohibition. The reason is that in 1611 this English word meant appropriate, suitable, or fitting, a meaning now obsolete. So also in the following.

Acts 24:25: "When I have a *convenient* season, I will call for thee."

Philem. 8: "I might ... enjoin thee that which is *convenient*."

These (like other instances in the King James) do *not* mean what we assume *convenient* means.

(6) *Conversation*. Everyone knows what this word means, right? Conversation is talking back and forth with others. So what about the following?

Psa. 50:23: "To him that ordereth his *conversation* aright will I shew the salvation of God."

Phil. 1:27: "Let your *conversation* be as it becometh the gospel of Christ."

This word occurs at least twenty times in the King James. Surely, by now, everyone reading this verse knows that it does *not* refer, specifically, to our words or to the way we talk. Instead, in this archaic usage—all twenty times!—the word means one's manner of living, behavior, conduct. (Which, of course, *includes* one's speech.)

(7) *Cousin*. In current English usage, this word refers to one's relatives who are immediately descended from a parent's sibling. Does that meaning apply to the following?

> Lk. 1:36: "Thy *cousin* Elisabeth, she hath also conceived a son."
>
> Lk. 1:58: "Her *cousins* heard how the Lord had shewed great mercy upon her."

Were Mary and Elisabeth, the mother of John Baptist, cousins? Maybe. Maybe not. In 1611, the word was used more broadly, for those descended from *any* common ancestor.

(8) *Doctor*. For us, this word refers to a medical doctor or one who has achieved the terminal degree in a given field of education—like a doctor of theology.

> Lk. 2:46: "They found him ... sitting in the midst of the *doctors*."

Many who read this verse will get the right idea in a general way, but they probably won't know that the word itself simply means *teacher*, which is its *original* meaning. Indeed, the Greek original has the very word that is usually translated *teacher*.

(9) *Halt*. We know very well that this word means stop, especially in (but not limited to) a military context where the troops are marching.

> 1 Kings 18:21: "How long *halt* ye between two opinions?"

We're likely to take this verse to mean that the people were stopping in between two opinions, going neither way, unwilling to commit.

And that wouldn't be *far* off. But the meaning here isn't quite that. Instead, *halt* has an archaic meaning no longer in use. It means to walk with a limp, hobble along. Sure, the people were not fully committing one way or the other, but they were hobbling along, trying to have it both ways. The difference is subtle, yes, but if one wants to know exactly what God said, this understanding is more precise.

Jer. 20:10: "All my familiars watched for my *halting*."

It might seem appropriate to take this word to mean that Jeremiah's acquaintance were watching for him to stop in confusion or discouragement. But, more subtly, they were watching for him, metaphorically, to limp or hobble: that is, to make a mistake in his prophetic utterances.

By the way, *halt* has this *obvious* meaning in Luke 14:21, where the lord in the parable commanded his servants to go bring in to his supper "the poor, and the maimed, and the *halt* [those who limped, were crippled], and the blind."

(10) *Instant*. We know what this word means, right? After all, we like our instant coffee or instant grits (if we like either one of those!). Instant means immediately, right away, no sooner said than done. But notice the following:

Lk. 23:23: "And they were *instant* with loud voices, requiring that he might be crucified."

If you're not careful, you'll take this word to mean that they immediately raised their voices to this end. But in 1611, *instant* had a meaning that's not usually recognized today: namely, urgent, pressing, insistent. The word also has this meaning in the following Biblical admonitions.

Rom. 12:12: "Continuing *instant* in prayer."

2 Tim. 4:2: "Be *instant* in season, out of season."

(I should say that urgent or insistent was the meaning the King James translators apparently intended. In these last two references the

Greek is different and some other meanings entirely might express the original intention more precisely.)

(11) *Meat*. These days, this English word refers to the flesh of an animal, like beef, pork, or chicken. That is not what the word meant in the English of the King James.

Lk. 24:41: "Have ye here any *meat*?"

In this case, since fish were involved, readers get the meaning about right, even if they don't understand that in 1611 this word meant food of any kind. In Hebrews 12:16, we read that Esau sold his birthright for "one morsel of meat," and we know from the original story that Esau was boiling lentils, not "meat" in our sense at all.

But there are many places where the word can easily be misunderstood. In the Old Testament (Leviticus 2, for example), the "meat-offering" was an offering of bread or its ingredients, like grain or flour.

(12) *Pitiful*. In current English usage, this word means to be the object of pity, to arouse pity from someone else. Consider the following.

1 Pet. 3:8: "Be *pitiful*, be courteous."

So should we obey this command by making ourselves objects of others' pity? Of course not! In 1611, the now archaic meaning of this word was to *show* pity or compassion to others. One who didn't realize this fact could probably figure it out from James 5:11: "The Lord is very *pitiful*, and of tender mercy."

(13) *Remove*. Here's a *re-* word that can fool us; see also the following word. In our usage, it means to take away, take off, do away with. And that's how most readers will take it in the following.

Prov. 22:28: "*Remove* not the ancient landmark."

This prohibition is bound to mean that we should not take away a property marker so that the boundary line is lost, right? Wrong! *Remove* is an older usage where remove simply means move: Don't *move* an old, established boundary marker. (People do that sometimes to make it seem that their property is larger than it really is.)

Sometimes, in the King James, *remove* means exactly what we would mean by it (as in Eccl. 11:10, for example), but sometimes it simply means to move from one place to another.

1 Cor. 13:2: "Though I have all faith, so that I could *remove* mountains."

At first reading, this word may seem to mean to take the mountains away entirely, but consider the words of Jesus in Matthew 17:20 that lie behind this verse, and it becomes clear that it means to *move* mountains from one place to another.

(14) *Replenish*. In current English usage, this word means to refill, to restock: in other words, to make full or complete again. Consider the appearance of this word in the following well-known verse.

Gen. 1:28: "God said unto them, Be fruitful, ... and *replenish* the earth."

It would be easy for a reader to take this verse to mean that the earth had previously been well populated and Adam and Eve were to begin the process of re-populating it. Indeed, some (uninformed) interpreters have taken it to mean this, claiming there was a race of people on the earth before Adam.

But in 1611, *replenish* had a meaning it no longer has: namely, to fill or supply completely—with no suggestion of doing so *again*. Note also Jeremiah 31:25: "I have satiated the weary soul, and I have *replenished* every sorrowful soul." That it means to fill or fully supply, here, is confirmed by the parallel statement before it; the Lord has not *re*-filled but simply filled the souls of the weary and sorrowing. Sure, the difference is not large, but we want to be precise in understanding the Word of God.

(15) *Unicorn*. In our use, this word refers to a legendary creature, a white horse with one ("uni-") long horn extending from its forehead. There is, and never was—should I say "probably"?—such

an animal. But the King James Bible refers at least nine times to unicorns.

Job 39:9: "Will the *unicorn* be willing to serve thee?"

Deut. 33:17: "His horns are like the horns of unicorns."

No, the Bible doesn't support the existence of unicorns. In 1611, this word meant a wild ox (or a similar animal; the Latin Vulgate sometimes rendered it with *rhinoceros*). My dictionary actually calls *unicorn* "a mistranslation of the Hebrew word."[16] But it wasn't a mistranslation in 1611!

Conclusion

One of the lessons of this chapter is that we ought always—regardless what version we read—to pay careful attention to the words of the Bible. All too often, people reading the King James (or some other version with words they aren't used to) read right past them without being conscious that they missed something. Mere reading isn't enough; we should *study* the Bible. And that includes getting help in understanding and interpreting it.

For my purposes in this volume, the important thing is to understand that the English of the King James is significantly different from the English that people write and speak in the twenty-first century. As I have shown in this chapter, that difference includes at least two categories: (1) the Elizabethan pronouns and verb endings that go with them; (2) many words that have different meanings, or no meanings at all, in our day.

Yet another difference, which I will not take space to develop here, is the matter of punctuation. The absence of quotation marks means that it is sometimes difficult to identify who is speaking. And

---

[16]The Hebrew word is *reem* (pronounced with two syllables, not one).

the usage of semi-colons and colons in the King James is very different from current English usage.

While we should not exaggerate the importance of these differences, neither should we underestimate them. Take the thirty words above, for example. They occur in *hundreds* of verses in the Bible, verses that modern readers might misunderstand or not understand at all. (And there are many more than these thirty.)

One has no choice, then, but to admit that the King James translation of the Bible does not use our language *as we use it*. In light of what I have said in the previous chapter, this difference is a matter of considerable significance. The Hebrew Old Testament used the Hebrew language as the people in Old Testament times used it. The Greek New Testament used the Greek language as the people in the days of Mark and Paul used it. The German translation of Martin Luther used the German language as people in Luther's world used it. The Wycliffe Bible used the English language as the English-speaking people in 1380 used it. The King James Version used the language as the English-speaking people in 1611 used it.

Indeed, that was the purpose of Wycliffe and Tyndale and all the other translators, including those who gave us the great King James. God intended for His Word to be in the language of people so they could read it and readily understand it.

Here's something you should consider. Anything written, say, above the heads of ordinary people, or using language in a way that is not familiar to them, stands at some "distance" from them. Apparently the Lord did not want His Word to be at a distance from those He gave it to. The closer a translation is to the people who use it, the more likely they are to understand it.

That is the very reason people have made translations in the languages people use.

CHAPTER SIX
The Original Preface to the King James Version

I include, in the following pages, excerpts from the preface to the King James Version of the Bible, as published in 1611. Since the previous chapter deals with the English of the King James Version, I think this chapter comes next.

The preface is especially instructive in showing the understanding that the translators had, as to the nature of, and reasons for, their work and the work of other translations. In that way, they provide exemplary instruction about the nature and role of translations for all of us.

I highly recommend the reading of these excerpts, at least. (The entire preface is available online; you may enjoy reading it all.)[17] Not only is this preface instructive, reading it may help one realize, even more acutely, how different our language was in 1611. All notes in brackets, [.....], are explanations I think may be needed for better understanding.

I have bolded some especially important observations and noted their significance.

---
[17]It appears on several websites. One is jesus-is-lord.com/pref1611.htm

The Translators to the Reader

Innovation Always Greeted With Resistance

Zeal to promote the common good, whether it be by devising any thing ourselves, or revising that which hath been laboured by others, deserveth certainly much respect and esteem, but yet findeth but cold entertainment in the world. It is welcomed with suspicion, instead of love, and with emulation [envious dislike] instead of thanks. **...For was there ever any thing projected, that savoured any way of newness or renewing, but the same endured many a storm of gainsaying or opposition? ...**

They understood that a new translation would be resisted.

Resistance to Innovation Always Aimed at the Most Important People ...

King James's Firmness of Purpose

This, and more to this purpose, his Majesty that now reigneth ... knew full well, accepting in the singular wisdom given unto him by God, ... That whosoever attempteth any thing for the publick, (especially if it pertain to religion, and to the opening and clearing of the word of God,) the same setteth himself upon a stage to be glouted upon [frowned on, scowled at] by every evil eye. ... Notwithstanding his royal heart was not daunted or discouraged for this or that colour, but stood resolute. ...

The Perfections of the Scriptures

But now what piety without truth? What truth, what saving truth, without the word of God? What word of God, whereof we may be sure, without the Scriptures? … In a word, it [the Scripture] is a panary [bread-supply] of wholesome food against fenowed [moldy] traditions; a physician's shop … of preservatives against poisoned heresies; a pandect [code of laws] of profitable laws against rebellious spirits; a treasure of most costly jewels against beggarly rudiments; finally, a fountain of most pure water springing up unto everlasting life. **And what marvel? The original thereof being from heaven, not from earth; the author being God, not man; the inditer [composer], the Holy Spirit, not the wit of the Apostles or Prophets; the penmen, such as were sanctified from the womb, and endued with a principal portion of God's Spirit;** the matter, verity, piety, purity, uprightness; the form, God's word, God's testimony, God's oracles, the word of truth, the word of salvation, etc.; the effects, light of understanding, stableness of persuasion, repentance from dead works, newness of life, holiness, peace, joy in the Holy Ghost; lastly, the end and reward of the study thereof, fellowship with the saints, participation of the heavenly nature, fruition of an inheritance immortal, undefiled, and that never

> They held a high view of Scripture.

shall fade away. Happy is the man that delighteth in the Scripture, and thrice happy that meditateth in it day and night.

The Necessity of Bible Translations

But how shall men meditate in that which they cannot understand? How shall they understand that which is kept close in an unknown tongue? ... Nature taught a natural man to confess, that all of us in those tongues which we do not understand are plainly deaf. ... Therefore as one complaineth that always in the Senate of Rome there was one or other that called for an interpreter, so lest the Church be driven to the like exigent [urgency], **it is necessary to have translations in a readiness.** Translation it is that openeth the window, to let in the light; that breaketh the shell, that we may eat the kernel, that putteth aside the curtain, that we may look into the most holy places, that removeth the cover of the well, that we may come by the water. ...**Indeed without translation into the vulgar [common, popular] tongue, the unlearned are but like children at Jacob's well (which was deep) without a bucket or something to draw with;** or as that person mentioned by Esay [Isaiah], to whom when a sealed book was delivered with this motion, Read this, I pray thee, he fain to make this answer, I cannot, for it is sealed.

They recognized the necessity of translations.

They recognized the necessity that translation be in the vernacular, the language of ordinary people.

The History of Bible Translations
Translations Into Greek

...The Greek tongue was well known and made familiar to most inhabitants in Asia by reason of the conquests that there the Grecians had made, as also by the colonies which thither they had sent. For the same causes also it was well understood in many places of Europe, yea, and of Africk too. Therefore the word of God, being set forth in Greek, becometh hereby like a candle set upon a candlestick, which giveth light to all that are in the house; or like a proclamation sounded forth in the market-place, which most men presently take knowledge of; and therefore that language was fittest to contain the Scriptures, both for the first preachers of the gospel to appeal unto for witness, and for the learners also of those times to make search and trial by. **It is certain, that that translation [the Septuagint] was not so sound and so perfect, but that it needed in many places correction; and who had been so sufficient for this work as the Apostles or apostolick men? Yet it seemed good to the Holy Ghost and to them to take that which they found, (the same being for the greatest part true and sufficient) rather than by making a new, in that new world and green age of the Church, to expose themselves to many exceptions and cavillations [trivial**

They recognized that the Septuagint, for example, was not perfect and yet was quoted by the New Testament writers as the Word of God.

objections], as though they made a translation to serve their own turn. ... Yet for all that ... it is evident ... that the Seventy were interpreters, they were not prophets. **They did many things well, as learned men; but yet as men they stumbled and fell.** ...

Translations Into Latin

There were also within a few hundred years after Christ translations many into the Latin tongue, for this tongue also was very fit to convey the Law and the Gospel by. ... But now the Latin translations were too many to be all good. ... Again, they were not out of the Hebrew fountain, (we speak of the Latin translation of the Old Testament) but out of the Greek stream [the Septuagint]; therefore the Greek being not altogether clear, the Latin derived from it must needs be muddy. **This moved St. Hierome [Jerome], a most learned Father, and the best linguist without controversy of his age, or of any other that went before him, to undertake the translating of the Old Testament out of the very fountains themselves; which he performed with that evidence of great learning, judgment, industry, and faithfulness, that he hath for ever bound the Church unto him in a special remembrance and thankfulness.**

They understood that translators are not inspired and work as human beings.

They understood what makes a good translator and had high regard for the Latin Vulgate, which Jerome translated from the Hebrew and Greek.

Translations Into Native Languages of Many Nations

… So that to have the Scriptures in the mother tongue is not a quaint conceit lately taken up … but hath been thought upon, and put in practice of old, even from the first times of the conversion of any nation; no doubt, because it was esteemed most profitable to cause faith to grow in men's hearts the sooner, and to make them to be able to say with the words of the Psalm, As we have heard, so we have seen.

Roman Catholic Resistance to Common-Language Translations …

The Present Translation Vindicated Against Objections to It

Objections Listed

Many men's mouths have been opened a good while (and yet are not stopped) with speeches about the translation so long in hand … and ask what may be the reason, what the necessity of the employment. Hath the church been deceived, say they, all this while? … Was their translation good before? Why do they now mend it? Was it not good? Why then was it obtruded to [forced on] the people? …

Objections Answered

… We are so far off from condemning any of their labours that travelled before us in this kind, either in this land, or beyond sea ... that we acknowledge them to have been raised up of God for the building and furnishing of his Church, and that they deserve to be had of us and of posterity in everlasting remembrance. ... Therefore blessed be they, and most honoured be their name, that break the ice, and give the onset upon that which helpeth forward to the saving of souls. **Now what can be more available thereto, than to deliver God's book unto God's people in a tongue which they understand? ... Yet for all that, as nothing is begun and perfected at the same time, and the latter thoughts are thought to be the wiser, so if we building upon their foundation that went before us, and being holpen [helped] by their labours, do endeavor to make that better which they left so good;** no man, we are sure, hath cause to mislike us. ... How many books of profane learning have been gone over again and again, by the same translators, by others? Of one and the same book of Aristotle's Ethicks there are extant not so few as six or seven several translations. Now if this cost may be bestowed upon the gourd, which affordeth us a little shade, and which today flourisheth and tomorrow is cut down; what may we bestow, nay, what ought we not to bestow, upon the vine, the fruit whereof maketh glad the conscience of man, and

> They understood the importance of having the Bible in the language one understands, and that later translations improve earlier ones.

the stem whereof abideth forever? And this is the word of God, which we translate. ... Therefore let no man's eye be evil, because his Majesty's is good; neither let any be grieved, that we have a Prince that seeketh the increase of the spiritual wealth of Israel. ... Let us rather bless God from the ground of our heart for working this religious care in him to have the translations of the Bible maturely considered of and examined. For by this means it cometh to pass that whatsoever is sound already, (and all is sound for substance in one or other of our editions ...) the same will shine as gold more brightly, being rubbed and polished; also, if anything be halting [limping, awkward], or superfluous, or not so agreeable to the original, the same may be corrected, and the truth set in place. ...

...We affirm and avow, that the very meanest [most mediocre] translation of the Bible in English, set forth by men of our profession ... containeth the word of God, nay, is the word of God: as the King's speech which he uttered in Parliament, being translated into French, Dutch, Italian, and Latin, is still the King's speech, though it be not interpreted by every translator with the like grace, nor peradventure so fitly for phrase, nor so expressly for sense, everywhere. ... A man may be counted a virtuous man, though he have made many

They understood that even ordinary translations are the Word of God.

slips in his life. ... **No cause therefore why the word translated should be denied to be the word, or forbidden to be current, notwithstanding that some imperfections and blemishes may be noted in the setting forth of it. For what ever was perfect under the sun, where Apostles or apostolick men, that is, men endued with an extraordinary measure of God's Spirit, and privileged with the privilege of infallibility, had not their hand? [That is, what was perfect except for that which was done under the hand of the Apostles?] ... The like we are to think of translations. The translation of the Seventy [the Septuagint] dissenteth from the Original in many places, neither doth it come near it for perspicuity, gravity, majesty. Yet which of the Apostles did condemn it? Condemn it? Nay, they used it, (as it is apparent, and as St. Hierome and most learned men do confess;) which they would not have done, nor by their example of using it to grace and commend it to the Church, if it had been unworthy the appellation and name of the word of God. ...**

They understood that the Bible is the Word of God when translated, even if human beings do not do so perfectly, that nothing is perfect except the original work of the inspired apostles.

They understood that the Septuagint translation differs from the original at times and is yet the Word of God.

Purposes and Procedures Underlying the Present Translation

...Truly, good Christian Reader, we never thought from the beginning that

They understood that they were improving

we should need to make a new translation, nor yet to make of a bad one a good one; ... but to make a good one better, or out of many good ones one principal good one, not justly to be excepted against; that hath been our endeavor, that our mark.
... And in what sort did these [that is, the translators of the King James Version] assemble? In the trust of their own knowledge, or of their sharpness of wit, or deepness of judgment, as it were in an arm of flesh? At no hand [not at all]. They trusted in Him that hath the key of David, opening, and no man shutting; they prayed to the Lord, the Father of our Lord, to the effect that St. Augustine did; O let thy Scriptures be my pure delight; let me not be deceived in them, neither let me deceive by them. ... Neither did we disdain to revise that which we had done, and to bring back to the anvil that which we had hammered; but having and using as great helps as were needful, and fearing no reproach for slowness or coveting praise for expedition, we have at length, through the good hand of the Lord upon us, brought the work to that pass that you see. ...

Some peradventure would have no variety of senses to be set in the margin, lest the authority of the Scriptures for deciding of controversies by the shew of uncertainty should somewhat be shaken. But we hold their judgment not to be so sound in this

good translations already existing.

point. ... **It hath pleased God in his Divine Providence here and there to scatter words and sentences of that difficulty and doubtfulness, not in doctrinal points that concern salvation,** (for in such it hath been vouched that the Scriptures are plain,) but in matters of less moment, that fearfulness would better beseem us than confidence. ... It is better to make doubt of those things which are secret, than to strive about those things that are uncertain. There be many words in the Scriptures, which be never found there but once, ... so that we cannot be holpen by conference of places. Again, there be many rare names of certain birds, beasts, and precious stones, etc., concerning which the Hebrews themselves are so divided among themselves for judgment, that they may seem to have defined this or that, rather because they would say something, than because they were sure of that which they said. ... Now, in such a case, doth not a margin do well to admonish the Reader to seek further, and not to conclude or dogmatize upon this or that peremptorily? For as it is a fault of incredulity, to doubt of those things that are evident, so to determine of such things as the Spirit of God hath left (even in the judgment of the judicious) questionable, can be no less than presumption. ...

They understood that some things remain uncertain, although not truth needed for salvation and Christian life.

Another thing we think good to admonish thee of, gentle Reader, that **we have not tied ourselves to an uniformity of phrasing, or to an identity of words, as some peradventure would wish that we had done.** ... **But that we should express the same notion in the same particular word [every time] ... we thought to savour more of curiosity than wisdom,** and that rather it would breed scorn in the atheist, than bring profit to the godly reader. For is the kingdom of God become words or syllables? Why should we be in bondage to them, if we may be free? use one precisely, when we may use another no less fit as commodiously? ... We cannot follow a better pattern for elocution than God himself; therefore he using divers words in his holy writ, and indifferently for one thing in name; we, if we will not be superstitious, may use the same liberty in our English versions. ... We desire that the Scripture may speak like itself, as in the language of Canaan, that it may be understood even of the very vulgar [that is, by the very common folk]. ...

They understood that there is more than one way to express the same meaning.

Conclusion

... It is a fearful thing to fall into the hands of the living God, but it is a blessed thing, and it will bring us to everlasting blessedness in the end, to listen when God speaks to us, to read his word when he sets it before us, and, when he stretches out his hand and calls, to answer, 'Here am I, here are we to do thy will, O God.' …

CHAPTER SEVEN
Translation: Understanding How It Works

In an earlier chapter, I dealt some with what's involved in translation. In this chapter, I want to come back to that subject and how translation works in creating different versions of the Bible.

Since I'm writing in English and for English-speaking people, I'm going to write in terms of the translation of the Bible into English. But what I say will apply to any language—except that we who speak English have a much larger variety of translations available to us than those who speak any other language on earth. There are a number of languages, like French and Spanish, that have several different versions to choose among, but none of them so many as English. Indeed, in English we have what might be called an "embarrassment of riches" available, in quantity and quality, compared to what is available in other languages of the world. We should be humbled by this advantage.

The Basic Problem of Translation

I have already said there is no such thing as a single set of words that can translate correctly from one language into another. What is said in one language can usually be rendered accurately by more than one set of words in another language. This flexibility doesn't mean that translation is arbitrary; the translator has to determine the meaning and then use words that convey that meaning.

No translation of the Bible is an exact expression of the original Hebrew/Aramaic and Greek originals. For that matter, no translation of *any* document in *any* language is an exact expression of it into another language. Languages just don't work that way.

Multiple Meanings for the Same Word

Any word in one language may have a meaning that can be translated by several different words in another language. Let me illustrate, first, by using the very first verb any beginning student of Greek learns: a verb meaning *to loose*.[18]

But there's more to it than that: *loose* isn't the only right or good way to translate this verb. It also, at times, means *destroy*.[19] Consequently, any translator has to *interpret* the context and decide whether the verb means one or the other whenever it appears. The decision isn't usually all that hard—but it's still a decision and the decision depends on what the word means *in a given context*. And the *context* simply means everything that's part of the sentence or paragraph or book that surrounds a word or group of words.

Start with two examples of this verb in the New Testament. (1) In Matthew 21:2 Jesus, using this verb, tells the disciples to *loose* the ass and colt and bring them to Him. Obviously, Jesus didn't want the animals *destroyed*.

---

[18] The Greek verb is λυω (transliterated *luō*). This form is the first person singular of the present active indicative, meaning *I loose*, which is the way Greek vocabulary is learned and the way it is listed in the Greek dictionaries/lexicons.

[19] There's a reason the same verb can have either of these two apparently different meanings, but we need not go into that here.

(2) In 1 John 3:8, we read that Jesus came to *destroy* the works of the devil, using the very same verb.

OK, that's simple enough, and easy to understand. But there is still more to this verb. There are other English words that can be used to convey the meaning of *loosing*, and there are other English words that convey the meaning of *destroying*. If you look up this verb in a Greek dictionary[20] it will give other English words as possible translations: *untie, set free, release* (which in a given context can accurately express the meaning of *loose*); or *break, break up, tear down, bring to an end, abolish, do away with,* or *annul* (which in a given context can accurately express the meaning of *destroy*).

For that matter, any other English words you can think of, that mean the same thing as *loose* or *release* could also be used; and any other English words you can think of that mean the same thing as *destroy* or *break* or *abolish* could also be used. As you can see, this flexibility means there are *many* possible English words that can be used in translating this Greek verb any time it occurs in the text.

I don't mean to say that the translator's choice of words is arbitrary or completely up to him or her. The translator has to use words that express accurately the *meaning* of the words he is translating, or else he would be irresponsible. Translating the Word of God is a serious responsibility.

Sometimes any one of several words would be equally good. For the ass and colt in Matthew 21:2, then, it would be fine to translate "untie them" (as in a number of versions), "free them," or "release them"—or anything else that means the same thing. 1 John 3:8 could read, just as correctly, that Jesus came to *abolish* or *do away with* the works of the devil. Any of these would be equally accurate, the Word of God.

---

[20]This is usually called a *lexicon*, showing Greek words and their English meanings.

But at other times there is a best word—or even the only word, occasionally—that will accurately convey the meaning in the context. And always the translator must be careful to determine the meaning in the context and choose the word that will best convey that meaning.

Here's another example, using the very same verb: 2 Peter 3:10-12. In verse 10 we read that in the Day of the Lord this world's elements will "melt" with fervent heat, and *melt* translates the same Greek verb. Now the verb doesn't literally mean *melt*, but in this context where the world is on fire, the King James translators chose the word *melt* to convey the idea of the destruction of the world. (Literally, the Greek says, "elements, burning, will be *destroyed.*")

Then, in verse 11, Peter says, "Seeing that all these things shall be *dissolved.*" And *dissolved* is the very same verb again. To be sure, dissolution is one way of being destroyed, and so the King James translators used this English word—twice, in fact.

So, we see, the KJV uses *dissolve* and *melt* to translate this verb. The ESV uses *dissolved* in all three places; the NIV and NASB use *destroyed* in all three. In my judgment, all three are equally accurate in conveying the meaning.

Here's another example using this verb. Luke 13:16 involves a woman who had been bent over for eighteen years and could not straighten up. After healing her, Jesus responded sharply to criticism: "Ought not this woman ... whom Satan hath bound ... be *loosed* from this bond on the sabbath day?" *Loosed* is the verb, and that makes good sense. Even so, the NASB reads: "Should she not have been *released* from this bond on the Sabbath day?" The NIV has "Should not this woman ... be *set free* on the Sabbath day?" Both of these are perfectly good translations. All mean the same thing and are equally accurate translations of the original Greek.

One more example. John 5:18 reports that the Jews sought to kill Jesus because, they said, He had *broken* the Sabbath. *Broken* is the same verb again. It certainly doesn't mean *loosed* or *freed*, here, but what exactly does it mean? Here's where interpretation gets involved—as it is everywhere, only sometimes more obviously than others.

Most interpreters, I think, take it to mean that He had broken Sabbath rules—violated the Sabbath—on that occasion; at least the versions I checked translate it that way. But some interpreters think (based on the entire Gospel of John, which is the larger context) that it means that by His action Jesus was *abolishing* or *annulling* Sabbath observance entirely. That would also be possible for this Greek verb. I would suggest that both ideas might have been involved, but I think it's wise to stick with *breaking*.

I have given this extended discussion of the ways of translating a single verb in the Greek New Testament, hoping you will see just how translation works. It isn't an arbitrary process. We don't just throw a bunch of words at people and let them choose any one they like best. I say, again: that would be irresponsible. But you do need to understand that words have multiple meanings and can be translated, correctly, in more than one way.

And I trust you also understand that I could do this same sort of thing with almost every word in the Bible. Translation works this way, and the flexibility shows up in different versions.

Multiple Meanings for Grammatical Forms

Now I want to use an entirely different illustration of the flexibility of translation, only this time I will illustrate with a grammatical *form* rather than a *word*. (Again, what I will describe could apply to almost every grammatical form in the Bible—and every phrase or clause depends on just such forms.

For my illustration I have chosen a favorite subject of mine, one I have explored in great depth in my own studies. I will use the Greek *participle*, which is much like our English participle. Since the usage of the participle form of a verb in Greek is similar in some ways to the usage of a participle form in English, I hope that my illustration will be relatively easy for you to understand.

For us, a participle is a verb form ending in *ing*.[21] In Greek, the participle has a particular form that is easily recognizable. Participles have many uses in Greek sentences, and I will zero in on one particular use: namely, a participle that expresses a secondary or subordinate action that is linked, in one way or another, to the action of the main verb in the sentence.[22]

Here's a made-up example: "*Dying*, Jesus purchased our redemption." *Dying* is the participle and that action is linked to the main clause, *Jesus purchased our redemption*. The question is, *how* does Jesus' dying relate to the purchase of redemption? Even in English, more than one answer to this question is possible.

This variety of possibilities also exists in Greek. Indeed, the Greeks used this sort of construction very broadly. In the New Testament such participles can be linked to the main clause *in any number of ways*. The action in the participle can express the *reason* or *cause* for the main action, or what happened *before* or *during* the main action (a *temporal* relationship), or the *means* by which the main action was accomplished, or even something *in spite of* which the main action took place (this use is called "concession").

Thus, my made-up sentence (whether in Greek or in English) *could* theoretically mean:

(1) "As He was dying, Jesus purchased our redemption."
(2) "Because He died, Jesus purchased our redemption."
(3) "By dying, Jesus purchased our redemption."

---

[21] Some such forms in English are gerunds, but we need not go into that.
[22] The technical name for this usage is a *circumstantial* or *adverbial* participle.

(4) "Although He died, Jesus purchased our redemption."

Or, for that matter, sometimes this kind of participle is only loosely linked to the main clause without a particular relationship being clear. In that case, it could be translated,

(5) "Jesus died and purchased our redemption."

How does the translator decide the meaning? I repeat: not arbitrarily. He or she simply considers everything in the context to determine, first, what it means, and then the best way to translate it so the meaning will be clear. That's the way translation works, and that's one of the reasons not all versions are worded in exactly the same way.

So let me give a real biblical example or two. I start with one very familiar to us, Hebrews 6:6. There, after a long set of clauses describing those who cannot be renewed to repentance, the writer gives this (in English): "seeing they crucify to themselves the Son of God afresh."

OK, watch closely. The Greek original simply says, "[they] *crucifying again* (these two words translate the participle) to themselves the Son of God." The question is, how does this adverbial phrase relate to the main clause? What does this participle have to do with the fact that it is not possible to renew to repentance the ones described?

Certainly, this participle—*crucifying again* (or *re-crucifying* or *crucifying afresh*)—explains the impossibility in some way, but how? The translator has to interpret the meaning, asking what makes best sense in the context. As always, context is the magic word.

The King James translators apparently believed it was the *cause* or *reason* for the impossibility. So they chose *"seeing* [that] they crucify." They could just as easily have rendered it *"because* they crucify." The NIV uses *because*. The NASB renders *since*, as do the NRSV and ESV. The NEB says *for*. All of these apparently regard the participle as stating the *cause* or *reason* these people cannot be brought back to repentance.

I think they are right. But that is a matter of interpretation, not "mere" translation. The Greek has nothing to indicate cause other than the most likely meaning *in the context*.

However, not everyone agrees with this understanding. Robert Shank, the author of *Life in the Son*, is convinced that the participle gives a *time* for the main clause rather than a *cause* or *reason* for it. Shank's view would render it thus: "It is impossible to renew them to repentance … *as long as* (or *while*) they are re-crucifying the Son of God." In other words, Shank does not believe that this apostasy is necessarily final; he believes that their renewal is impossible only so long as they continue in their denial of Christ.

The Greek construction alone does not tell us which is right. We have to depend on the context. Again, the decision is not arbitrary, the translator must objectively decide which fits the context. And sometimes, two translators may come to different conclusions, both of them being equally conscientious.

There are hundreds of these participles in the New Testament. Here's the kicker, and it's an important point, so don't miss it. Shank's temporal translation *could* be the Word of God—*but only if that is what the original, inspired text intended.* Personally, given what the next verse says, I tend to doubt that Shank's reading is what the Holy Spirit (or the writer of Hebrews) intended, and I tend to trust the fact that the published translations I've checked read it as expressing a cause or reason.

Even so, keep this principle in mind: *The thing that determines whether any translation is the Word of God is whether it accurately expresses what the original, inspired text intended to express.* See, that isn't up to translators; they are bound by what the text says and means.

I give just one more example of this kind of participle in the New Testament, this one from Romans 9:11-12. There Paul is saying, about Jacob and Esau even before they were born, that (in the words of the King James) "The children *being* not yet *born*, neither *having done* any good or evil,... it was said unto her [Rebekah, their mother], The elder shall serve the younger." There are two of these participles in this sentence, *being born* and *having done*.

I begin by copying several different versions of these same words for you. And, by the way, comparing translations is an excellent way to discern the interpretive issues in a given verse or passage.

—Literal Greek: [Them] not yet being born nor doing anything good or bad ... [it] was said to her."

—ESV: "Though they were not yet born and had done nothing either good or bad ... she was told."

—NIV: "Before the twins were born or had done anything good or bad ... she was told."

—NRSV: "Even before they had been born or had done anything good or bad ... she was told."

—NASB: "Though the twins were not yet born, and had not done anything good or bad, ... it was said to her."

You will notice that two of the four translations use *though*, the other two use *before*. Those using *though* (which could have been *although* or *even though*) took the two participles to express what we call "concession": that is, something in spite of which the main action took place: even though Jacob and Esau had not yet been born and had not yet done anything good or bad to deserve any distinction between them, in spite of that the Lord told Rebekah that the older (Esau) would serve the younger (Jacob).

Those using *before* took the two participles to express a relationship of time: Even before the twins were born or had committed any acts of their own to deserve any distinction between them, the Lord said Esau would serve Jacob.

Now some reader might say, in response to this observation, that one of these is right and the other one wrong. Perhaps, but not necessarily. Either one fits the context. In this instance, *either one entails the other*—which is not always true, but is true here. What God said about the two boys was both before and in spite of the fact that they had not been born yet. Either translation is accurate.

I am not saying, of course, that every difference is so easily explained. Sometimes, the way such a participle in Greek is interpreted or understood by one translator may be different in meaning from the way another translator understands (and translates) it—as in Hebrews 6:6, above.

You may notice that the King James translators avoided having to make a decision about Romans 9:11-12 by translating the Greek participles as English participles. That's not a bad decision; doing it that way leaves it to the English reader to ask and decide what it means, just as the Greek reader must decide. Sometimes the King James translators left the participle uninterpreted, but more often they expressed the interpretation in the translation, as they did in Hebrews 6:6. And other translations do the same things, at times.

And what I've said about participles in Greek can also be said about many other grammatical forms in that language.

Summary: How Honest Translation Can Lead to Different Versions

In summary, there are several things to remember here, as follows. There is no way to avoid different possibilities, since all translations (as I have indicated in an earlier chapter) are the work of human beings doing the best they can—as human beings serving the Lord—to discern the meaning of something in writing in one language and then to translate with that same meaning in another language.

(1) There is usually more than one accurate way to translate, even when exactly what the original means is absolutely clear and all translators agree.

(2) At times there is room for more than one understanding of what the original means, and then there will be differences in translation that reflect these differences in understanding.

(3) Furthermore, there are differences of opinion about the best method of translating the Bible (or anything else)—different philosophies of translation, in other words. I will not take time to explain these differences here but will return to this matter in a later chapter. For now, I will simply say that some translators prefer a stricter approach that can be described as literal or word-for-word. (I may say that I think the Bible-believing view of *verbal* inspiration, described in chapter one, tends to provide good grounds for a word-for-word approach, in general.) Others prefer a less strict approach that can be described as free or thought-for-thought. These differences are not absolute, and any version can be either of these, more or less. These different approaches also lead to different versions. (There are also even freer approaches that lead to what we call *paraphrases* rather than strict translations. They introduce more interpretation into the text.)

(4) In all translation decisions, the work of translation is not arbitrary or subjective. Although the words and grammatical forms are flexible, they also have bounds, and translators must work within those bounds. Translators must be honest and objective, work hard to determine the meaning of the text in the original languages, and then work just as hard to render the text in the languages of the translations to communicate accurately.

The Choice of Words in Translations

In the first chapter in this book, I emphasized, as I emphasize again now, that the inspiration of the original writers of the Bible included divine superintendence of the very words chosen, since words are important ways of expressing ideas precisely. That's what we call *verbal* inspiration.

Since Moses and David and Jeremiah, and Matthew and Paul and James wrote under that supernatural influence, there have been thousands of translators of the Scriptures, translating them into thousands of languages all over the world, as I have explained in chapter two. While the Christian church has never claimed the miracle of inspiration for the translators, yet God has preserved His Word through them for peoples everywhere.

Yes, the translators choose the words best suited to convey the meaning of the original writings. And they do so as human beings. At the same time, we expect them to do their work in dependence on the Holy Spirit, and we are confident that those who truly depend on the Spirit will receive His help. And, just as the King James translators realized, later translators may well improve the translations of earlier ones, especially as the language changes or as they learn more.

This seems a good place to illustrate the role of translation of the Bible in contrast to the way Islam views its holy book, the Koran. Muslims have such a view of the dictation of the words that they simply do not permit translation at all. Every faithful Muslim must learn Arabic in order to read the *true* Word of God, as they view it. Christianity not only allows but encourages human beings to translate the Scriptures, being confident that we can adequately convey the meaning of the original by a different set of words in a different language.

By the way, what I've said about God-fearing translators is likewise true for God-fearing preachers and teachers and writers of commentaries—*and laity*! All of them are handling the Word of God that He gave us to be responsible for.

Let me illustrate what I've just said. In our denomination alone there will be perhaps 2,000 sermons preached, by 2,000 different preachers, in our churches on any given Sunday. They will be "preaching the Word of God," we trust. *They* will choose the words they use; that is a *human* work. We trust they will depend on and be led by the Spirit of God in doing so, but in some—yes, many—cases, their choices of words could be improved.

In the same way (with an important exception I will add), the God-fearing persons who have given us translations of the Bible in our languages do their work. They, too, are human beings, and they have not been miraculously caused to do such perfect work that no improvement is possible.

The exception is that the best translations we have are made by large *groups* of God-fearing persons who know their business well and are sincerely committed to being objective in translating the Scriptures. This kind of translation is one of the ways God has preserved His Word for us. I will come back to this matter in the final chapter.

Why Verbal in the Original and Not in the Translations?

What I've just said may raise a question. Some readers may think it is strange that I would insist on *verbal* inspiration of the originals and not insist on exactly the same thing for translators. Well, there are reasons for this insistence.

For one thing, the Bible itself speaks of the inspiration of the Scriptures. It doesn't say anything about translators. And, when you think about it, it doesn't need to. Once we have a verbally inspired original, then we have all we need. God works, from then on, through human beings who have that original as a baseline by which to evaluate every manuscript and every translation. He holds us responsible, as human beings through whom He works, to guard and keep His Word, to make sure that the Bibles in our hands accurately speak what He spoke through the inspired writing prophets and apostles.

That is the reason it is so important to understand the *original writers were controlled by the Holy Spirit. It is important to have an inspired Word to go back to.* Since the original words were chosen under the supervising influence of the Spirit of God, we have an authoritative original, and we humans can check every translation we have against those words. And since the accuracy of a translation depends on *meaning*, we can know we have the inspired Word of God when we have the same truths conveyed, with the same meaning as the original, in another language—including ours.

That is the way *any* translation is to be evaluated. *Every* translation gives us the inspired Word of God *to the extent that it accurately communicates what God originally said.*

I realize that someone may raise the question, how can we go back to the original, inspired writings since we don't have the original sheets on which the inspired writers (or their scribes) wrote? That leads us into the next chapter.

CHAPTER EIGHT
What About Manuscript Differences?

Why do some recent versions have words that aren't in the King James or lack words that are in the King James? While some of those differences are simply differences in translation (see the previous chapter), many of them are because of differences in the manuscripts. I've already explained, in chapter two, about the thousands of Greek manuscripts we have, and the fact that they were made by hand by scribes, so differences exist. As I said before, no two of the manuscripts (those of any significant size) are 100% alike in every word or letter.

My purpose in this chapter is to show how these differences are handled in various versions, and here I feel more challenged in explaining what's involved in a way that every reader can understand. This subject is very complex and involves technical terminology; but I will avoid the technical terms as much as possible and try to explain in a way that the average layperson can understand.

First I repeat a point I made earlier: the copyists were not advantaged with the same supernatural overshadowing that the prophets and apostles experienced. They did their work as human beings. For the most part, they were conscientious and careful. In the monasteries, where copying was regarded as a sacred occupation, there were methods used to try to avoid mistakes. Even so, differences in the copies arose and were re-copied in later manuscripts.

Where Do We Start?

Start by remembering that *we do not possess the original work of the Bible writers.*

This fact is not surprising. The originals would have been handled so much that they would have been too worn to survive. In those days the people would not have had printing or photocopying to have such written materials in their own possession.

Consider 1 Thessalonians, for example. Even at Thessalonica, where this letter from the honored apostle was received, it would have been read aloud to the whole congregation assembled—no doubt treasured and re-read aloud many times.

Other churches would have learned that Thessalonica had a letter from the great apostle, and they would have asked for a copy, and one would be made. There's no telling how many copies were made by other churches. Within a short period of time, the letters of the inspired apostle would soon be regarded as appropriate for the churches everywhere. And in those churches, too, the copies would be read aloud for all the believers to hear.

The same thing can be said for the four Gospels and Acts, as they made their appearance, and for the rest of the New Testament. That same thing had already begun, long before, in regard to the Old Testament in the Jewish synagogues scattered all over the civilized world where Jews had migrated.

In other words, the process of making copies would have started early and spread rapidly. So, even though we don't have the originals, we have copies—probably copies of copies of copies, and we can't be sure just how many "generations" of copies there were between the originals and any copies that exist now. First Thessalonians was written by Paul about the year A.D. 50. The earliest manuscript of 1 Thessalonians that still exists was probably made, as some think, during the period between A.D. 125 and 225, thus during the second or third centuries—from 75 to 175 years after the original was sent from Paul to Thessalonica. We have no way of knowing whether it was copied from the original or from a copy of a copy of a copy of the original.

That's the way things are with all the New Testament. All the originals were written before A.D. 100, and the oldest manuscripts we have are from a century or so later. Indeed, we don't have very many manuscripts that old. But we do have enough to compare and be sure we can tell just what the original text contained.

What Manuscripts Do We Have?

Perhaps you've heard it said that there are over 5,000 manuscripts of the Greek New Testament in existence. Yes, and there are at least that many more Latin manuscripts and manuscripts in other languages like Syriac and Coptic. I do not mean there are 5,000 manuscripts of the *whole* New Testament, but 5,000 that contain at least *some* of the New Testament. Some of these are scraps, containing only a few lines; some are of a single book of the New Testament, like Romans or Mark; some contain a group of books, like Paul's epistles; only some contain the *entire* New Testament, and fewer still contain the whole Bible.

You will understand that the farther away from the time of Christ one gets, the more manuscripts there are. Only a relatively small number of the manuscripts that have survived were made within the first few centuries of the Christian era. Many more from the period 500 to 1500 have survived, and even within that millennium there are more later than earlier ones. This distribution is exactly what you would expect.

Also obvious is the fact that later copies, generally speaking, have more generations of copies between them and the originals, allowing more opportunity for differences to creep in. Common sense tells us that copies made in 1500, as compared, say, to copies made in 500, were generally more likely to be made from late copies.

Was the Process Entirely Human?

I have emphasized that the process of copying was a work of human beings. Was not God at work, providentially, in this process?

Yes, He was. The providence of God encompasses *everything* that happens, and we read the hand of providence *after the fact*. We can only tell what providence has done by looking to see what has actually transpired. (For more discussion on this matter, see the following chapter.)

So, in the providence of God, we have all these thousands of copies, which differ from each other. And two things can be said. First, and most important, *they are so much alike that it is clear that God has providentially preserved His Word in them*.

Second, they do differ, and *we humans have to be the ones to sort out those differences and determine which ones are most like the originals*. There simply isn't a way to avoid this responsibility. In His providence, God uses human work. The scribes who copied the Scriptures—including those in Catholic or Greek Orthodox monasteries—and the men and women who now compare these manuscripts in order to determine which ones most accurately represent the originals are all part of the way God works providentially through the agency of human beings.

There are no halos, no signs from God, on any of the manuscripts to identify them as the most accurate ones. In His providence, they have all come to light in the same ways, by human effort, using carefully developed methods that are public. Providence gives us exactly what we have, and we have to work with that.

So What About the Differences in These Manuscripts?

The question is obvious: now that we have all these manuscripts, which differ, what do we do about that?

One thing we *don't* do is to magnify these differences. What's really encouraging—and an evidence of God's hand in things—about the different manuscripts, is that, by and large, *they are alike*. You could choose almost *any* New Testament manuscript and use it and have all the same doctrines and practices. (Of course, choosing a single manuscript isn't the way to deal with the differences.)

What we *do* is simple: we do our conscientious best, seeking the assistance of the Spirit of God, to determine (by all the means and abilities God has given us) which manuscript(s) have the original words, one verse at a time.

This work requires specialists, scholars who spend their lives in training and in practicing their craft. It is a field of study that requires years of education and an almost single-minded devotion to continuing research. These textual scholars, as I'm going to call them,[23] have to learn how to recognize the habits of scribes, the forms of writing in use at different periods of history, and many other things they need to evaluate manuscripts.

Here's a short and non-technical way of summarizing what these textual scholars do: they compare manuscripts and make discerning judgments, word by word, as to what the original had. They attempt to make critical judgments, at any given place in the manuscripts

---

[23]The technical term for them is "textual critics," and their field of expertise is "textual criticism." These terms do *not* mean they "criticize" the text, but that they compare the manuscript differences and make critical judgments as to which wording is most likely to match the original, inspired wording.

where there are differences, to determine which ones more likely match the original.

There is a lot more to it than that, of course, and I won't try to give extensive details. They try to date the manuscripts accurately, since older ones are closer in time to the originals. They try to establish where the manuscripts were made, since that can help in evaluation; if manuscripts made in different locations agree in a given wording, that strengthens the scholars' confidence in that wording. They classify manuscripts by their tendencies, such as whether some scribes tended to add clarifying details, for example. They group them into families that share common readings and tendencies. They look for patterns in the differences. And so on, all of which helps them do their work objectively.

I repeat, then, that they exercise their scholarly abilities in order to decide, word by word, what the originals of Paul and Moses and the others said.

Then, when they have done their work, publishers use their decisions as a basis for producing printed Greek New Testaments. And, finally, the translators use these printed texts to translate the New Testament into English—or into any other language.

It's that simple, and it's that complicated.

All Versions Are the Result of Using These Methods

I trust you will understand, then, that *every single version of the Bible available to us is the result of this kind of work.* Early, those who published Greek New Testaments, like Erasmus, soon after printing was available, had only a few, relatively late manuscripts to compare. Even so, Erasmus was his own textual scholar. He compared the dozen or so manuscripts he had, to see where there were differences in wording. He made decisions as to which words matched the original. Then he published a Greek New Testament.

Afterwards, then translators used that Greek New Testament to translate into other languages, including the early English versions like the King James.

It is not possible for any translator to translate from the original documents, since they no longer exist. All translations use texts that result from the careful comparison of manuscripts and the human decisions as to which of those differences is more likely original. Because this work is so dependable, scholars are confident that in almost every word, we have the original text in the published Greek New Testament.

I repeat: this work is done in publishing versions of the Bible in English or in other languages. The nature of this work has not changed and will not.

Seeing This Work Accurately

The work of the textual scholars is never done; it continues to this day, and I want to make three important points here, about the way they work.

(1) Generally speaking, the textual scholars and translators are *not* influenced by bias against the supernatural or Bible-believing Christian doctrine.

The textual scholars do not have an axe to grind in exercising their judgment about differences in manuscripts. This work or comparison and judgment goes on both for biblical manuscripts and for manuscripts of other ancient documents, according to established methods. The textual scholars are not trying to make the Bible, or any other document, read in any certain way. They have no agenda other than to try their best, objectively, to determine what the original had.

It doesn't matter to them, for example, that the biblical writings present Jesus as God or set forth supernatural things like the Virgin

Birth and miracles. They are well aware that the Bible teaches such things. Some of the textual scholars may not personally believe such things themselves, but they are happy that the Bible writers believed them—even if they think those beliefs were silly superstitions. They do not make a conscious effort to remove such things from the Bible.

(2) Textual scholars and translators do not decide to omit certain things from the Bible. Let me explain what I'm saying with an illustration, using Colossians 1:14. The King James says, "In whom we have redemption *through his blood*." But the Greek text produced by the textual scholars, and the translations that are based on this text, do not have the words "through his blood" in this verse.

Please understand: the translators of the recent versions did not decide to omit those words; the Greek text they were translating did not have the words. The textual scholars didn't decide to omit the words; they were looking both at manuscripts that had the words and at manuscripts that didn't have the words. And they simply decided, based on all the methods and tests they use, that the ones without the words matched what Paul originally wrote in Colossians. I'll come back to this matter below, but by the way the majority of the manuscripts do not have those words in Colossians 1:14.

Neither the textual scholars nor the translators wanted to make a case against the blood of Christ in redemption. They know very well that the New Testament writers believed that redemption was by the blood of Christ, and they don't mind that (whether they themselves believe it or not). If *they* were trying to remove blood redemption from the New Testament, they would do a much more consistent job of that than just "omitting" it from Colossians 1:14. They simply and honestly don't believe, based on the evidence, that those words were in the original of Colossians 1:14 as Paul penned (or dictated) the epistle. And the majority of manuscripts, early and late, agree with them that the phrase was not there.

(3) Majority doesn't rule. One cannot simply tell what the original said by counting all the manuscripts and determining what the majority of them have. That, of course, would be an "easy way out." It would be a way for humans to avoid having to make a decision at all: just count and let the majority of the manuscripts decide.

It ought to be easy for any reader, thinking carefully, to know that majority does not determine originality. If, say, there are twenty-five manuscripts which have a certain word, that only argues that the *one* copy from which they were made had it, and that *one* may not be any better than another single *one* that doesn't have that word. Indeed, suppose the *one* that doesn't have it was copied in the year 300, and the 25 that have it were copied in the year 1000 or later, then indeed the one that doesn't have it may very well be more dependable than the twenty-five that do.

There are many things, in other words, that are more important than how many manuscripts read the same way. These include things like the *age* of the manuscripts, the *patterns* shown by the scribes who copied them, the *sources* of the manuscripts, and so on. The work of the textual scholars *has* to be done, and we who are not textual scholars have to depend on them. We simply don't have any alternative, unless we just arbitrarily pick something to put our confidence in.

How Did Differences in Manuscripts Happen?

There isn't space, here, to delve into this subject in great detail, but you may find it helpful to think about how the scribes produced manuscripts that differ. Let me illustrate by using Colossians 1:14 again. Either Paul wrote the verse without "through his blood" or he wrote it with "through his blood." If the former, then some scribe added the words. If the latter, then some scribe left them out. (And then it doesn't matter, you see, how many copies were made from each.)

How could a scribe add them if they were not originally there? There are numerous ways an addition could happen. Perhaps the scribe who was making this particular copy was familiar with other New Testament passages that say "through his blood"—like Ephesians 1:7, which has the very same truth: "In whom we have redemption through his blood." Without even realizing he was doing it, he might have added "through his blood" from his memory of the other passage.

Or perhaps he thought that surely the copy he was copying had accidentally left it out, and so he added it. Or perhaps he (or someone else, later) just put it in the margin as a comment, based on Ephesians 1:7; then a later scribe, copying it, thought the marginal note was meant to be part of the text and added it in.

If those words were originally in Colossians 1:14, it is equally easy to understand how some scribe might have accidentally left them out, not even realizing that he missed them. Often when copying something of great length, by hand, we lift our eyes from the page where we're writing back to the text we're copying and accidentally skip something, especially if the sentence makes sense without what we skipped—as it does here in Colossians.

Such is the nature of the human work of copying manuscripts by hand. Technically, then, we may not be absolutely sure whether the words "through his blood" were in the original of Colossians 1:14 or not. But this possibility does not disillusion us. We lose nothing if they are not there, since the necessity of the blood is clear elsewhere, as in Ephesians 1:7. (By the way, if some ungodly "scholar" were trying to take the blood out of the New Testament, he would probably have removed the phrase from Ephesians 1:7, too!)

Most important, Christian doctrine and Christian practice are unaffected whether the words are in Colossians 1:14 or not. (I'll have a more complete illustration about the blood of Christ in the New Testament below.)

Here is something important to me: if the presence of this phrase in Colossians had been absolutely necessary for us to get the truth of this passage and of the New Testament, then I'm confident that God, in His providential preservation of His Word, would have seen to it that we would not have any ambivalence about it. I am sure we have the Word of God, here, whether we read those words in the verse or not.

Interestingly, as I noted, these words are *not* in the majority of the Greek manuscripts of Colossians, and the ones that don't have them include the oldest manuscripts. Modern translators and textual scholars haven't left them out; some early scribe either left them out or added them.

I repeat: whatever manuscripts you put confidence in, the basic truths of the Christian faith—for doctrine and practice—are the same.

The Greek Texts Available to Translators

If you want a Greek New Testament to translate, for all practical purposes, there are three possibilities.

(1) One can choose to use the same text that Erasmus published and that was used by the King James translators in 1611. This is called the "Received Text."[24] It was first published in 1516 and some relatively minor revisions were made during the years that followed, notably the edition of Stephanus in 1550 and that of Elzivir in 1621. (This latter is *technically* "the Received Text.")

Perhaps you will find it helpful to know that Erasmus, at the time he produced his Greek New Testament, had access to about a dozen

---

[24] Often called by the Latin equivalent, *Textus Receptus*, typically abbreviated as *TR*.

Greek manuscripts and the Latin Vulgate. None of the Greek manuscripts was older than the tenth century, and none contained the entire New Testament. Only one contained the book of Revelation. In a few places, when none of his Greek manuscripts contained things in the Vulgate, he translated from the Latin into Greek. It's interesting, however, that in spite of the limited materials available to him, compared to the thousands of manuscripts available now, he was aware of most of the textual differences. That might have resulted, in part, from his familiarity with the Latin manuscripts and versions.

(2) One can choose what is called the "Majority Text." As the name suggests, it represents the majority of the Greek manuscripts. These, for the most part, are a large number that were made under the sponsorship of the Greek Orthodox Church, mostly during the Middle Ages. Such a text had not been published, as such, until 1982. It is very close to the Received Text in most of the New Testament, but there are numerous differences throughout the New Testament and especially in the Book of Revelation. As far as I know, no English version of the New Testament has been published as a translation of this edition of the text.

(3) Or one can choose what is called a "critical text." This is a text that is published as a result of the work of the textual scholars I've described above. They compare all the manuscripts and make critical judgments as to which wordings are most likely to match the originals.

Over the years, scholars have published various editions of the critical text as their knowledge and skills have developed (and, for that matter, the text of Erasmus was a "critical text" in its day). The one published by B. F. Westcott and F. J. A. Hort in 1881, which also went through several revisions, is no longer thought to be the best. These days, the work of textual scholars shows up in the latest (of several) editions published either by the German Bible Society[25] or the United Bible Societies. As of now these two publish the same Greek text. This text serves as the basis for many modern translations. These days, this text does not enjoy the monopoly it had in the past, and other groups of textual scholars are publishing equally dependable editions of the critical text. Interestingly, all of the editions available show a high degree of agreement.

Illustrations From the New Testament About Manuscript Differences

It's time, now, for me to provide some examples of the manuscript differences *as they show up in different versions*. I am referring to differences that actually affect wording. There are many differences that do not affect wording, as in spelling, for example. But I will deal only with variations that could make a difference, say, between the Received Text, used by the King James and New King James, and the critical text used by some other versions. These will serve to illustrate the things I've been explaining above. I will only give a few of many possibilities, but other illustrations would be similar.

(1) 3 John.

I begin with a short little book of one chapter, so the reader can see the differences in a whole document. (Again, there are many differences that don't affect words, as I've just indicated.) Of about 220 words (in the critical Greek text), only ten words might be different from the text translated by the King James—which amounts to less than five percent. (Throughout the New Testament, the textual schol-

---

[25]This edition of the text is often referred to by the initials NA, standing for scholars Nestle and Aland.

ars believe they can be sure of all but about one percent, but that is difficult to quantify or determine precisely.)

Verse 4. King James: "I have no greater joy than to hear that my children walk in truth." Some manuscripts have "the truth," others just "truth." The textual scholars, these days, think "the truth" is probably original (although the evidence is mixed), and so the contemporary versions read that way. (Actually, versions might differ in this instance merely by translation; even without *the* in the Greek text, the word *truth* can correctly be translated "the truth."

Verse 5. King James: "whatsoever thou doest to the brethren, and to [the] strangers" (there is a "the" with "strangers" in the Greek being translated). This way, John appears to mean two different groups that Gaius (the recipient of the letter) had been kind to.

Some manuscripts have an additional word (literally "this"[26]), and no article with "strangers," literally, "whatever you do for the brothers, and this for strangers." This way, John appears to mean *one* group that Gaius had been gracious to, his action especially appreciated since they were brethren who were strangers to him.

Verse 8. King James: "We therefore ought to receive such," where "receive" translates a fairly common Greek verb with this meaning. Some manuscripts have a slightly different Greek verb[27] (one letter different) that means *receive as a guest, support*. The ESV and NASB use "support," while the NIV has "show hospitality to."

Verse 9. King James: "I wrote unto the church." Some manuscripts have an additional pronoun[28] that means "something," which shows up in the NASB and ESV but not in the NIV. (The NIV translation, however, might have resulted from translation theory rather than from a textual difference.)

---

[26]Greek *touto*.
[27]Greek *hupolambanein* rather than *apolambanein* in the Received Text.
[28]Greek *ti*.

Verse 11. King James: "He that doeth good is of God: but he that doeth evil hath not seen God." Some manuscripts (both the older manuscripts and the majority) do not have the conjunction "but,"[29] and so the newer translations use a semi-colon or period instead.

Verse 12. King James: "Ye know that our record is true." Some manuscripts have singular "you know"[30] instead of plural. The newer versions probably mean *you* singular, but since they use *you* for singular or plural, one is not able to tell the difference.

Verse 13. King James: "I had many things to write, but I will not with ink and pen write unto thee." In the Greek translated by this verse, the first "write" is present tense and the second is aorist tense,[31] while in some manuscripts the two tenses are reversed. But this difference does not necessarily affect translation.

As you can easily see, only one of these actually makes any difference in *meaning*. That is the one in verse 5, where it is difficult to be sure whether Gaius had given aid to one group (brethren who were strangers to him) or two (brethren and strangers). For that matter, either of the two readings could mean either of the two meanings.

And, more importantly, Christian doctrine and practice are not affected by any of the differences.

(2) Some selected passages.

I would not pretend that all the differences in manuscripts are as inconsequential as those in 3 John—although *most of the differences have no importance at all*. Here are some examples of the kind that seem more significant.

- Romans 16:5, in the King James, identifies Epaenetus as "the firstfruits of *Achaia*." But some manuscripts have "the firstfruits of

---

[29]Greek *de*.
[30]Greek *oidas* instead of *oidate* in the Received/Majority text.
[31]Greek *graphein* and *grapsai*, respectively.

Asia," which is contained in the critical text and followed by modern translations. (*Asia* is in the older manuscripts, fewer in number; *Achaia* is in the majority, mostly later.) As similar as the words are, with just a letter or two different, it is easy to understand how some scribe, perhaps listening to dictation, might have got it wrong, either way.

Here the textual scholars are confident that *Asia* was in Paul's original. We who are not textual scholars (including me!) can make our own decisions, of course, although we aren't as well equipped to do so. Perhaps we will choose to live without being absolutely sure which province Epaenetus was the first convert from—Acts doesn't tell us.

But it is important to realize that this manuscript difference, like nearly all manuscript differences in the New Testament, makes absolutely no difference in any matter of Christian doctrine or practice. So our God did not preserve the original word, here, in 100% of the manuscripts. Providence has given us manuscripts with *Asia* and manuscripts with *Achaia*; and human beings have to decide which is probably original—or remain undecided.

That is the way things are with some of the manuscript differences.

• There are a very few larger blocks of material that are affected by manuscript differences. Perhaps the two largest are the so-called long ending of Mark (16:9-20) and the story of the woman taken in adultery (John 7:53—8:11). I will comment briefly on each of these. (Interestingly, even Erasmus knew about them and expressed his doubts.)

The Gospel of Mark ends at 16:8 in two of the oldest and most highly regarded Greek manuscripts and in another one or two. Nearly all other Greek manuscripts that contain Mark include verses 9-20. Furthermore, verses 9-20 are not in some of the manuscripts of some of the oldest versions in other languages or as Mark is quoted in some of the early church fathers.

So the textual scholars think verses 9-20 were probably not in the original Gospel composed by Mark. That some uncertainty remains may be indicated by the fact that our modern English versions (I checked ESV, NIV, and NASB) include these verses but provide a note to the reader about the fact that some of the earliest manuscripts do not include them. (Some of the critical Greek texts do the same thing.) (Or they might have chosen to include the passage for the sake of tradition.)

Whether these verses were original or not has been debated a long time, and arguing one way or another would be beyond my purpose here. Personally, I am satisfied they were original; but any meaningful decision should ultimately result from careful consideration of the evidence. At the same time, it is important to realize that there is nothing in these verses that adds to or takes away from what is revealed to us about Christian beliefs and practices.

For that matter, there is nothing in these verses that adds to the information we have (in the other Gospels and Acts) about the days following Jesus' resurrection (except for the part about handling snakes and drinking deadly poisons, in verses 17-18). My confidence in the Bible as the very Word of God remains the same either way. If these verses were not original, then we would have another case of human work that the Lord in His providence allowed to become part of the manuscript tradition.

The situation with John 7:53—8:11 is similar, except that in this case a larger number of Greek manuscripts (and other sources, like ancient versions and writers) do not contain the verses, including those same two very old ones. The textual scholars, again, are more or less confident that this account of the woman taken in adultery was not in John's original Gospel. (Still, some of the versions include the account but provide a note for the reader. They might have included the passage this way for the same of tradition rather than because of uncertainty, however.)

Everything I've said about the ending of Mark can be said again here. There is nothing in this passage that either adds to our understanding of the gospel, and of Christian doctrine and practice, or is against the spirit of what we know about Jesus and His teaching and works. Indeed, many commentators are confident that the account is both old and true, even if it wasn't originally in John. (I have a sermon on this passage that I am not hesitant about preaching, and I do not raise doubts about its place in the Gospel.) The fact that the Bible is the Word of God is not at stake in this matter.

You will understand (as I've already said) that neither the textual scholars nor the translators of the modern versions "decided to omit" these passages. These passages simply are not in the manuscripts that the textual scholars believe match the original, inspired text. That may seem to be a way around the problem, but it is an important thing to understand, lest one "demonize" people who do not deserve it.

(3) The deity of Christ.

Are the editors of the critical Greek text, or the translators of our modern versions, biased against some basic Christian doctrines?

One of those doctrines is the deity of Christ, and an important indicator of this truth lies in the fact that Jesus is sometimes directly called *God* in the New Testament. Do the manuscript differences or the modern versions show any bias here?

Using any of the Greek texts, there are eight or nine places in the New Testament where the word "God" *may* be applied directly to Jesus. Only two of these involve manuscript differences.

The first place is John 1:18, where the majority of the manuscripts call Him the *Son*—as the KJV translates. But the older manuscripts (essentially the same few that omit the two long passages discussed above) call him *God*. And so the textual scholars, being consistent, believe John's original said "the only begotten *God*." And the newer versions translate with *God*.

The second place is 1 Timothy 3:16, where the KJV, translating the Received Text, says "*God* was manifest in the flesh." But some of the older manuscripts have the relative pronoun *who* instead, which the textual scholars believe, as they read the evidence, was original; and the newer versions translate with a pronoun.

So if one chooses the critical Greek text instead of the Received Text, or the versions that translate them, he will add one place and subtract one place where Jesus is called God. That is neither a gain nor a loss. And the manuscripts and newer versions agree with the King James and the Received Text in affirming that Jesus is God in the other places. (Except that, in fact, the King James translation is ambiguous in Titus 2:13 and 2 Peter 1:1, where the translation (God *and* our Savior) could mean either two persons or the same person; the newer versions translate, unambiguously, "our God and Savior, Jesus Christ."

It seems clear, then, that there was *not* at work any effort to downplay the deity of Christ—neither in the manuscript differences, nor in the textual scholars who compare manuscript differences and decide what wording was probably original, nor in the translators who translate the latter.

I once read someone who thought there was some tendency in the modern versions to downplay the more honorific names by which Jesus is called, such as Lord or Christ. I did a study of Galatians and Ephesians, comparing the KJV and the NIV, as a way of checking this usage. I found no basis at all for thinking that there is any such tendency. The name *Christ*, either by itself or in tandem with *Jesus*, appears 77 times in each of those two versions. The tri-fold name *Lord Jesus Christ* or *Jesus Christ our Lord* appears 11 times in the

KJV and 10 in the NIV. (The few differences are all manuscript differences, not arbitrary decisions of the translators.)

(4) Redemption by the blood of Christ.

I've already mentioned Colossians 1:14. The question is whether the manuscripts themselves—or the textual scholars who specialize in them, or the translators—show bias against the blood of Christ as the means of our redemption? This possibility can easily be checked.

In the KJV, representing the Received Text, there are 32 references to the blood of Christ as the means or basis of our salvation or sanctification or redemption (and in a few similar expressions). Interestingly, the NIV, representing the critical text, has the blood of Christ in *all* of these places except for Colossians 1:14, as dealt with above (where even the majority of Greek manuscripts do not have the phrase). Obviously there was no sinister effort afoot to take blood redemption out of the New Testament.

Here is the list of references to the blood of Christ that I have counted: Matt. 26:28; Mk. 14:24; Lk. 22:20; Jn. 6:53-56; Acts 20:28; Rom. 3:25; 5:9; 1 Cor. 10:16; 11:25, 27; Eph. 1:7; 2:13; Col. 1:14, 20; Heb. 9:12, 14; 10:19, 29; 12:24; 13:12, 20; 1 Pet. 1:2, 19; 1 Jn. 1:7; Rev. 1:5; 5:9; 7:14; 12:11; 19:13.

I should probably note that at least one translation of the New Testament—*Today's English Version*, translated by Robert Bratcher[32]—intentionally changes many of the New Testament references to the blood of Christ to the *death* of Christ. While it is true, as Bratcher insisted, that the shedding of Christ's blood was another way of referring to His death, yet in the Bible the shedding of blood for sacrifice had a deeper meaning not conveyed by the simple word *death*. Jesus' death was a *sacrificial, atoning death*.

---

[32] Also known as *Good News for Modern Man*.

(5) The personality of Satan

Do the newer versions play down the personality of Satan by omitting reference to him by name? Again, this possibility can be easily checked. In the King James Bible, representing the Received Text (in the New Testament), the name of Satan occurs 55 times. In 53 of those 55 places, the name of Satan appears in the NIV, representing the critical text (in the New Testament).

The two places where the name Satan does not appear are interesting. The first is Psalms 109:6, where the NIV translates the Hebrew word for Satan as "an accuser" rather than as *Satan*. What makes this translation interesting is that there are seven other times in the Old Testament where the KJV does the very same thing that the NIV does, translating this same Hebrew word either as *adversary* (six times) or as *one who withstands* (one time). So the NIV translators did eight times what the KJV translators did seven times; it's difficult to see any conspiracy in that. By the way, the Hebrew word for Satan *means* an adversary or accuser.

The other place is in the New Testament, in Luke 4:8, where a manuscript difference is involved. In the KJV, the first part of Jesus' answer to the devil (at the temptation) is, "Get thee behind me, Satan." These words are not included in those older manuscripts I have mentioned, and the textual scholars believe they were not in Luke's original. So they do not appear in the critical text and therefore the translators of more recent versions, using that text, do not have them.

I would say about this difference the very same sort of thing I have said about other manuscript differences above, such as whether Epaenetus was from Asia or Achaia (Rom. 16:5). You should know that it *is* clear that these words *were* said by Jesus and are included in the parallel account in Matthew 4:10. So nothing is lost to us as a result of the fact that some manuscripts do not have them in Luke 4:8. (If some scribe, or textual scholar, or translator wanted to remove the name of Satan from Jesus' lips, he would no doubt have left them out in Matthew as well as in Luke.)

Conclusion

I think I have provided enough examples of manuscript differences, which show up in editions of the Greek New Testament and in translations. I believe the examples serve to demonstrate the various kinds of things that may be involved. I think they also tend to show that those differences are *mostly* of little or no consequence. And the ones that seem more significant make absolutely no difference in any item of Christian doctrine or practice. God has preserved His Word in all the ways we needed it to be preserved. For more on this subject, see the following chapter.

CHAPTER NINE
Confidence in Our Bibles: The Providence of God and the Preservation of His Word

As I begin to conclude this little volume, I am aware that some skeptics will continue to doubt the Scriptures. They may say something like this: If the scribes made errors in copying the Scriptures and the various manuscripts do not entirely agree, then we have no settled Word of God to place our confidence in.

My purpose in this chapter is to show that such a view is nonsense. There are many convincing reasons for trusting our Bibles as the Word of God. Here are just some of them.

The Manuscripts and Translations Agree in Spite of Their Differences

This point is the most important of all, and it is clear testimony that God has preserved His Word. *Everything our God wanted to teach us in His Word has been preserved and is clear in spite of the differences in the copies and translations.* If because of manuscript differences, for example, we aren't quite sure whether Jesus went to Gadara or Gergesa (Matt. 8:28; Mk. 5:1; Lk. 8:26, 37), we still know exactly what the Word is teaching us in those passages. Jesus' deliverance of the demoniac is the same in all the sources.

As I have said often in this work, no item of Christian doctrine or conduct is at stake with any of the differences in manuscripts or standard translations.

There are many, many things that are essential to the Christian faith. Many doctrines are included in our cherished—and saving—beliefs. I could list the entire gamut of theological truths here. There is a personal, infinite God who is omnipotent, omniscient, and omnipresent—as well as perfectly holy and loving. He eternally exists, without change, as Father, Son/Word, and Holy Spirit. He sent the Son to become one of us by being born of the Virgin Mary. The Son, in His perfections, took on Himself the guilt of our sins and bore that guilt before God the Father who "laid on him the iniquity of us all" until He was satisfied, reconciling us to God. All who have faith in Him as their Savior and Lord are saved and destined for eternity with Him. Those who reject Him are separated from Him and tormented forever.

No matter what manuscript tradition you use, these doctrines are clearly taught. Furthermore, all the manuscripts confirm that we are saved by grace through faith, and that we should be baptized and join a local church where we attend regularly. Also, we should practice the things that Jesus taught us, and these are not left for us to guess at.

Even in our denominational differences we have the same Word of God. If we believe that washing the saints' feet is an ordinance to be practiced, what the Bible says to convince us of this ordinance is the same in all the texts. If we believe that one who has been born again can turn from God and become unregenerate, we will find this doctrine in our Bibles. And those who differ with us will find their grounds in their Bibles, which say the same things as ours!

True Christians agree on all the essential doctrines, and all the Bibles they use teach those doctrines. They disagree on many less essential things, and that comes about in spite of the fact that the Bibles of all of them teach the very same things about those matters.

When it comes to practice, these same conclusions apply. All who believe the Bible will agree that it is a sin against God and others to worship idols, to commit murder or adultery, to lie or steal or covet—because all the Bibles they use teach those things clearly. They disagree about how to apply some of the biblical principles to specific practices that people disagree about, like certain entertainments or manner of dress—or (in Paul's day) whether believers should eat food that had been offered to idols—and if so, in what circumstances. But these differences aren't because their Bibles differ; their Bibles say the same things.

In other words, the only differences that depend on differences in copies are differences that we don't have to know about. Nothing we need to know about doctrine or behavior is any different because of the variations in manuscripts or translations.

If I had nothing else to cling to, this fact alone would let me rest my confidence in the Bible as the Word of God in exactly the way it has come to us.

The Magnitude of the Witnesses to the Word of God

The Bible has far more ancient copies, to testify to its content, than any other writings from antiquity.

No one is surprised that since the invention of printing the things that have been put into print—in huge quantities—are reasonably safe from errors. A popular writer, these days, may sell a million copies of his book, and they all say exactly the same thing. No one doubts whether the book of any given author contains his words. He turned in his manuscript (whether handwritten or as an e-copy) to the publisher. The typesetter put it in print and sent a copy to the author to proofread. Others proofread it too. A very few typographical errors might escape notice, but by and large the book contains just what the author said.

Before printing, however, writings were published as hand-written copies, and that process isn't quite so near-perfect as modern publishing. The number of copies made depended primarily on demand. All ancient writings were preserved this way, and for most of them there are multiple copies. For Homer's *Iliad*, for example, written about 900 B.C., there are less than 2,000 manuscripts in existence, at least at the last count I have seen. The oldest one dates to about 400 B.C., thus 500 years after the original was written. And the manuscripts agree closely but not perfectly. There is no good reason to challenge the idea that we have Homer's word.

By comparison, there are more than 5,000 manuscripts of the Greek New Testament, the earliest one dating to less than a hundred years after the New Testament was written. Those manuscripts also agree, to a high level. (And there are many more thousands of manuscripts in other early translations like the Syriac, Coptic, and Latin.)

And Homer's *Iliad* is the ancient writing that's best attested, next to the New Testament! For writers like Pliny, Plato, Herodotus, and Thucydides, for examples, there are less than a dozen manuscripts of each that still exist.

In other words, the New Testament manuscripts are far more numerous than for any other ancient documents. And their basic agreement with each other testifies to the great care with which they were produced and demonstrates their accuracy. The small number of disagreements, and the fact that those disagreements don't create doubt about essential doctrines and practice, should silence even the noisiest critic of the Bible.

We have the Word of God in our hands as it was written by the original, divinely-inspired authors and conscientiously translated into our language. A person may reject the Bible as the Word of God, of course—many people do—but the manuscript differences won't provide an adequate grounds for that rejection.

Indeed, most who reject the Bible do so for other reasons. To such reasons we would respond with the traditional defense of the Bible as the Word of God: its reliability, its consistency, its accurate speaking to the human condition, its claims, its effectiveness, its coherent answers to the most important questions of life—and so on.

But if anyone questions the Bible because of the manuscript differences, we will answer that it is the ancient writing whose manuscripts make it the best-attested such writing in the history of the world.

Understanding the Providence of God

I'm going to emphasize that God has preserved His Word in the work we call *providence*. I've mentioned the matter of providence a couple of times already. I think that almost every Christian thinker calls on providence when describing how God has preserved His Word. Generally speaking, providence is God's more "ordinary" work, not involving miracles.

It is important, therefore, to understand God's providence. There isn't space for a full discussion of providence here; that is something I've tried to do a little more thoroughly elsewhere.[33] But we can summarize some major truths about this important doctrine.

Providence can be defined, simply, as the activity of God by which He provides for the created order. This activity includes His preservation, care for, and governing of it, and the created order includes the physical universe, plants and animals, and human beings.

---

[33]See "Toward a Non-Deterministic Theology of Divine Providence," *Journal for Baptist Theology and Ministry* (online journal of New Orleans Baptist Theological Seminary), 2014.

God's providence includes everything that transpires. Nothing is outside the realm of His supervision and government. Consequently, as one popular song put it, "He's got the whole world in His hands." And "everything that transpires" includes good and evil. Romans 8:28 confirms that He works *all things* together for the ultimate good of those who are His.

His providence is seen in His provision for His creatures, including speechless animals. Psalm 104:10-31 is especially powerful in describing this provision. Providence is likewise seen in the function of the laws of nature. And God's providence is at work in His management of the circumstances of our lives, even when those circumstances include our own mistakes and bearing the consequences of them. This working of the circumstances of our lives is sometimes called *special* providence.

We can only read the hand of providence *afterward*. We can only tell how He has worked when He has worked. *We* don't get to pick which circumstances we like as providential. All we can do, finally, is gather all the facts and do our best to determine how we see God at work in them. And we aren't infallible in making such determinations.

It is easy to acknowledge God's providence when He brings us, without our arranging it, to the very thing that meets a need—to the doctor who recognizes an illness and knows just how to treat it, for example. It isn't quite so easy, however, when an armed burglar invades at night and kills one's child. Even so, God's providence is at work in *all* the circumstances of our lives.

In other words, we are just as much responsible, when we try to understand the ways of God, as we would be if we didn't mention providence. That doesn't mean, of course, that we are agnostics about providence. I, for one, am often able to attribute some benefit I experience to the providence of God—and, right or wrong, thank Him for it. But I repeat: I know I'm not infallible in this recognition, and that I must finally acknowledge His providence in *all* the circumstances. When my wife died, I felt that God providentially arranged for all of my daughters to be with me in the room. Well, yes, but it was also in His providence that she died.

How, then, do we apply the doctrine of the providence of God to the preservation of God's Word? To begin with, it should be clear that we can't be selective in attributing just a part of history to the providence of God. Not just the preservations of *some* of the manuscripts. Not just a certain translation, like that of Luther, or the King James in 1611. In the end, the doctrine of providence offers no help in deciding between the versions of the Bible. We have neither the right nor the ability to look at all the events, in the history of how the Bible has come to us, and select the ones we personally like as the ones by which He has preserved His Word.

In other words, *everything* involved in our discussion, in the previous chapters, has taken place in the providence of God. In His providence, we have thousands of manuscripts of the Bible and they don't perfectly agree in every word and letter; and yet they agree in every essential matter of Christian faith and practice. In His providence, we have people who carefully study those manuscripts and do their best to determine, word by word, which words match the original, inspired text. In His providence, we have thousands of people who take the results of those textual scholars and do their best to translate from the original languages into the languages of everyday people. As in everything else in our circumstances, then, *we* are left to interpret the significance of this or that manuscript, this or that translation, this or that version. Such is the way God works, providentially, in the lives and work of human beings.

What I've just said doesn't cancel the confidence expressed in the rest of this chapter or in chapter one. In faith, we remain certain that God has preserved His Word and that He has done so as part of His providential government of our world. Even so, He has left it to us, using our resources—under His leadership, we trust—to read the evidence and reach God-honoring conclusions.

Conclusion: How God Has Preserved His Word

In light of all the discussion, then, I would venture these brief statements about how God has preserved His Word.

(1) He preserved it by the miraculous work of inspiration, exercised by the Holy Spirit on the original writing prophets and apostles.

(2) He preserved it by prompting the church to recognize and respect the inspired writings as the Word of God. (This preservation, then, includes the matter of canonicity[34]—of the writings that effectively forced their way into the recognition of the church and correctly make up the Bible.)

(3) He preserved it by providing for many scribes, over thousands of years, to make careful copies of the originals, and then copies of the copies, and copies of the copies of the copies for many generations.

(4) He preserved it by prompting many leaders of the early church to write many good things in which they quoted and commented on many biblical passages, thus giving us even more evidence as to what the originals said.

(5) He preserved it by prompting many early Christians, whose languages were different from those of the original writings, to make translations that have likewise been copied and preserved, including the Syriac, Coptic, Latin, and others.

(6) He preserved it by cleansing the church in the days of the Protestant Reformation, which once again directed the attention of

---

[34] We speak of the Bible as a whole as the *canon* of Scripture. The *canonicity* of the 66 books that are there means they are the very ones that belong there because God intended them to be there and providentially guided the church to recognize that they (and no others) belong there.

God's people to the Bible itself and fostered the work of putting it into their hands.

(7) He preserved it by raising up Gutenberg to invent movable type and make possible the mass distribution of the printed Word.

(8) He preserved it by raising up scholars to compare different manuscripts and publish a resulting text, only the first of these being the Roman Catholic Erasmus who compared the dozen manuscripts he had and published the first Greek New Testament, which was used by early Protestant translators like the translators of the King James and others.

(9) He preserved it by raising up dedicated scholars, soon after the Reformation began, to translate the Bible into other languages: like Luther into German and others into French, Spanish, English, and ultimately a thousand other languages.

(10) He preserved it by leading dedicated researchers—like Constantin von Tischendorf and others to the present day—to find, publish, and collate thousands of manuscripts, many of them much older than the ones available in the Middle Ages, to confirm further the wording of the original.

(11) He preserved it by leading dedicated specialists to follow in the steps of Erasmus, to the present day, and continue the work of comparing manuscripts to determine as accurately as possible the wording of the originals.

(12) He preserved it by raising up yet other scholars, to the present day, to follow in the steps of the Protestant reformers and keep up the work of translating the Bible into the languages of people all over the world.

(13) He preserved it by raising up Bible-believing scholars to write commentaries on the Bible to explain its meaning more fully, and Bible-believing preachers and teachers to proclaim and expound the Bible as the Word of God.

That isn't all, of course. But you get the idea.

A Concluding Observation

I am aware that there will be some Bible-believing folks who find that what I have said is not enough. They are not satisfied with the fact that every matter of Christian doctrine and practice will be the same across the difference manuscript traditions and versions, or that God has preserved everything essential for us with certainty. For them, nothing less than 100% certainty about every single word is required. They cannot accept that manuscripts differ, so that one version says Jesus went to Gadara and another version that He went to Gergasa; or at least they cannot accept that both of these versions are the Word of God in our hands. They cannot even be satisfied with differences in translation: if one version says "Mary was pledged to be married to Joseph" and another says "Mary had been betrothed to Joseph," then as they see it both can't possibly be the perfect Word of God.

For them, then, there is no alternative but to pick a certain version and regard that version *only* as the Word of God. Theoretically, such a person could pick the Geneva Bible, or the King James, or the New American Standard. Or the Latin Vulgate, or the French *La Bible de Jèrusalem* (The Jerusalem Bible), or some other. If any such choice is made, the chooser must then do two things: justify making that choice when there is no Bible teaching that points to it; and explain how the choice they have made relates to the possibility of having the Word of God in any other language, including our language as it is currently in use in real life.

CHAPTER TEN
Some Practical Suggestions

In this chapter, I want to conclude, briefly, with some practical suggestions you may want to consider. You have choices and you're the one who will make those choices. You need to do so with as much information and understanding as possible.

The King James

Perhaps you want to stick with the King James. I won't criticize that option. It's tried and true, represents (although not entirely) a word-for-word approach to translation, and in the New Testament is based on the Received Text (the Greek New Testament first published by Erasmus 500 years ago, with some revisions).

If you decide to make the King James your primary Bible to read, I hope you'll view that as a *preference* and not because you think it's the only true Word of God. I hope you won't feel spiritually superior to folks who make a different choice.

You do need to understand that there are words in the King James that can trip you up, not to mention the strange-sounding pronouns and verb endings of Elizabethan English (see chapter five). You can get used to the latter, but you will need some help with the words that are out of date.

For such reasons I would suggest that you supplement reading the King James by reading some other good version or commentary. You need to know when clarification of the meaning of a word is needed. And reading another version can give you additional insight into what God has said to us. I won't keep repeating this advantage, but it is true regardless what version you use.

The New King James

If you want a version that simply updates the outdated words and uses contemporary pronouns and verb endings, you may want to try the *New King James*. Technically, it is not a new translation but an updating of the King James. This version uses the very same text in the original languages—the Received Text in the New Testament—that the King James uses, and it expresses the same translation philosophy. These things may appeal to you. This way, you will probably ignore those places where manuscripts differ. And if your background is the King James, the New King James will sound familiar.

Furthermore, some editions of the New King James include footnotes that will inform you about the places where the manuscripts have differences, and you can learn more about those.

Other Versions

Perhaps you want to use some other version for your primary reading—other than the King James or New King James, that is. That means there will be a number of options, and there are some things you will want to keep in mind in order to make a sound choice. Here are some brief suggestions.

(1) Be aware of the different philosophies or methods of translation. Some versions are more word-for-word, while others take more freedom with the words in order to provide thought-for-thought

translation. Reading the preface to a version should help you understand the translation philosophy used in it.

There is more than one way of describing these differences. Instead of word-for-word and thought-for-thought, some use the terms *literal* and *free*. Some use the more technical terms *formal equivalence* (using the same grammatical forms as the original) and *dynamic equivalency* (striving for equivalent meaning rather than grammatical form). Another approach I've seen uses *formal* versus *functional*, in about the same way. None of these distinctions is absolute and no version is entirely one or the other. All versions, including the King James, are at some point between one end of the spectrum and the other end. Some are closer to a conservative, word-for-word approach, and some are closer to a freer, thought-for-thought approach.

Read the preface and ask for advice from experienced believers. Prefer versions used widely by Bible-believing Christians, which may be called "standard" versions. Some people may tell you that there is a connection between believing in the inspiration of the *words* and a word-for-word philosophy of translation. But, as I've said before, the true basis for judging a version lies in its accuracy in rendering the *meaning* of the original, not in the precise words used in translation.

(2) Consider the translators. Always prefer a translation produced by a large and representative group over one produced by one or a few individuals. The group influence tends to avoid individual biases or personal idiosyncrasies. It yields greater objectivity.

Also, always prefer a translation produced by Bible-believing Christians rather than those whose theology is suspect. You won't want to use the *New World Translation* of the Jehovah's Witnesses, for example.

(3) Don't make a paraphrase your primary Bible. A paraphrase is a step beyond a translation that takes even greater liberties in *interpreting* the text. A paraphrase tends to express the meaning of the

original in a way that can be very different from the way it was originally expressed. It may add nuances of interpretation that are not in the original at all.

Here's an example. In 2 Kings 9:30, the text says that Jezebel "painted her face, and tired her head." Nothing in the text says *why* she did this. One paraphrase says she "posed *seductively* at the window," which is pure interpretation. Perhaps she was trying to be seductive, but some interpreters think, instead, that she was proudly facing the death she knew was imminent. (By the way, "tired" is another of those Elizabethan words that don't mean the same thing anymore.)

A paraphrase may be useful, but if so its use is similar to that of a commentary or a sermon based on Scripture. Some of the more well-known paraphrases by evangelicals are *The Living Bible* and *The Message*.

(4) Again, then, you may want to consider reading regularly from more than one version. Reading carefully and evaluating as you read will be good for you. You shouldn't accept a new idea just because it's innovative. Reading more than one version can give you fresh insight into the meaning. (But if the meaning in one differs radically from another, you should be careful and exercise critical judgment.)

Indeed, here's an idea if you're open to other versions: try a parallel Bible which has, say, from two to four versions side by side. That way, you can compare for yourself.

I'm not going to recommend any certain versions, but I will name some of those that seem most widely used. I'll offer brief suggestions about them and place them on a line according to the translation philosophy, ranging from more word-for-word at one end (named first) and more thought-for-thought at the other (named last). The differences between the most useful of these are not all that large.

—The *New American Standard Bible* (NASB). Faithfully (but not entirely) word-for-word; but the English usage is not as current or readable.

—The *English Standard Version* (ESV). More word-for-word than thought-for-thought.

—The *Christian Standard Bible* (CSB), which started out at the Holman Christian Standard Bible. Announced as word-for-word when readable, but more dynamic when required to make it more readable.

—The *New International Version* (NIV), which I see as about midway between word-for-word and thought-for-thought.

—The *New English Translation* (NET), which is primarily an internet version; it also tries to strike a balance between literalness and readability.

—The *New Living Translation* (NLT), which has been developed from *The Living Bible*, a paraphrase. It isn't as much a paraphrase as its predecessor but is near the border between translation and paraphrase. It is more thought-for-thought than word-for-word.

—The *Message* (MSG), which is a true paraphrase.

Whatever you do, read your Bible carefully and with a desire to meet God in His Word. God has spoken, and you have His Word in your hands. Get it in your heart. Let your mind be shaped by it. Learn to think like God thinks.

That is the way you can know the will of God. He has revealed Himself and the way you can know Him and please Him.

Thy word have I hid in mine heart, that I might not sin against thee. (Psa. 119:11)
Thy word is a lamp unto my feet, and a light unto my path. (Psa. 119:105)
For ever, O Lord, *thy word is settled in heaven. (Psa. 119:89)*

www.ingramcontent.com/pod-product-compliance
Lightning Source LLC
Chambersburg PA
CBHW070159100426
42743CB00013B/2977